NATIONALISMS AND NATIONAL IDENTITIES

CONTENTS

Editorial	**1**
Women, Nationalism and Islam in Contemporary Political Discourse in Iran *Nahid Yeganeh*	**3**
Feminism, Citizenship and National Identity *Ann Curthoys*	**19**
Remapping and Renaming: New Cartographies of Identity, Gender and Landscape in Ireland *Catherine Nash*	**39**
Rap Poem: Easter 1991 *Máighréad Medbh*	**58**
Family Feuds: Gender, Nationalism and the Family *Anne McClintock*	**61**
Women as Activists, Women as Symbols: A Study of the Indian Nationalist Movement *Suruchi Thapar*	**81**
Gender, Nationalisms and National Identities: Bellagio Symposium Report *Catherine Hall*	**97**
Culture or Citizenship? Notes from the 'Gender and Colonialism' Conference, Galway, Ireland, May 1992 *Clara Connolly*	**104**
Reviews	
Kate Soper on *The Politics of Truth*	**112**
Maria Lauret on *The Woman at the Keyhole: Feminism and Women's Cinema* and *Issues in Feminist Film Criticism*	**114**
Clare Whatling on *Inside/Out: Lesbian Theories, Gay Theories*	**117**
Peggy Watson on *Polish Women, Solidarity and Feminism*	**118**
Judith Squires on *Dimensions of Radical Democracy* and *Engendering Democracy*	**120**
Linda McDowell on *Destabilizing Theory: Contemporary Feminist Debates*	**123**
Letter	**126**
Noticeboard	**129**

Feminist Review is published three times a year by a collective based in London, with help from women and groups all over the UK.

The Collective: Alison Light, Avtar Brah, Ann Phoenix, Annie Whitehead, Catherine Hall, Clara Connolly, Dot Griffiths, Erica Carter, Gail Lewis, Helen Crowley, Lola Young, Loretta Loach, Lorraine Gamman, Lynne Segal, Mary McIntosh, Naila Kabeer, Razia Aziz.

Corresponding editors: Kum-Kum Bhavnani (currently resident in the US), Sue O'Sullivan (currently resident in Australia), Ann Marie Wolpe (currently resident in South Africa).

Correspondence and advertising
For contributions, books for review and all other correspondence please write to:
Feminist Review, 11 Carleton Gardens, Brecknock Road, London N19 5AQ.
For advertising please write to:
David Polley, Routledge, 11 New Fetter Lane, London EC4P 4EE

Subscriptions
Please write to: Subscriptions Department, Routledge Journals, Cheriton House, North Way, Andover, Hants SP10 5BE.

Contributions
Feminist Review is happy to discuss proposed work with intending authors at an early stage. We need copy to come to us in our house style with references complete and in the right form. We can supply you with a style sheet. Please send in 4 copies plus the original (5 copies in all). In cases of hardship 2 copies will do.

Bookshop distribution in the USA
Routledge, Chapman and Hall, Inc. 29 West 35th Street, New York, NY10001, USA.

Typeset by Type Study, Scarborough

ISSN 0141-7789

APOLOGY
We would like to apologize to Jody Sealwood as we omitted to credit her for the photographs of Catherine Arthur's drawings which were published in *Feminist Review* 41, Summer 1992.

Transferred to Digital Printing 2004

EDITORIAL

It is a sombrely appropriate time to be considering the issue of nationalism, with the bloody disintegration of a once-stable, multi-national Yugoslavia. As we go to press, we hear terrible stories of the systematic rape of Muslim women in Bosnia, involving not only physical violation, but forcible impregnation. This is the most grotesque re-minder of how, fundamentally, nationalism is gendered – women's bodies are the boundary of the nation, and the bearers of its future.

This issue of *Feminist Review* is not so much about the history of nationalist *movements* (nor their political outcomes) as about national *ideologies*, i.e. the cultural resources that nationalisms bring to the creation of a common identity. All national ideologies are gendered: most commonly, women are the *symbol* of the nation, men its *agents*, regardless of the role women actually play in the movement. Variants of the theme run through almost all the articles here, although they describe very different nationalist movements – in Iran, India, Ireland, South Africa, Australia and imperial Britain.

Suruchi Thapar describes how this process worked in India: Hindu female icons were used to represent the nation as passively feminine (toning down the warlike aspects of some, like Kali, a symbol for the more oppositional women's groups). She gives an account of the construction of ideas about femininity and womanhood in pre-indepen-dence India, the crucial ways in which they structured liberation ideologies, and also how they circumscribed the role of women in the nationalist movement.

Catherine Nash illustrates how – in representations of the land-scape of the West of Ireland in the early twentieth century – the nation's space (the land) is feminized, against the 'masculine' colonial power. In opposition, she places the work of Kathy Prendergast, contemporary Irish artist, who – reworking the trope 'landscape/woman' – uses the metaphor of 'mapping' to expose both the colonial appropriation of land and male control of the female body. Máighréad Medbh, in 'Easter 1991', subverts the traditional image of 'Eire' as long-suffering mother, awaiting rescue through the action of her loving sons. Medbh's 'Ireland' is sick – yes, sickened as much by her own men as by the colonial invader – but she is active, and impatient.

Anne McClintock examines the gender–blindness of some of the standard academic writings on nationalism. She explores several potent metaphors of woman/family/nation, with (she demonstrates) long historical roots. The nation as family, she argues, is a figure for sanctioning social hierarchy within a (presumed) unity of interests. In this light, she compares Afrikaaner and ANC nationalisms.

Ann Curthoys describes recent attempts to forge a more inclusive, multicultural Australian identity, in reaction to the strong critical voice of Aboriginal men and women, and the challenge that they present to republican as well as to more traditional ideals of nationhood. Changing the focus from 'nation' to 'state', she then argues that the relationship between contemporary feminists and Australian state institutions has been a productive one; she defends the notion of 'citizenship' against its feminist critics.

Nahid Yeganeh traces the different implications for women of the secular, 'modernizing' nationalist movement, and the more recent Islamicization of the state, in Iran. She explores the inconsistencies of the latter project, in a modern state which requires the presence of women in the public sphere, particularly in education.

Finally, we carry reports of two successful conferences on the subject – one organized by *Gender and History* and held in Bellagio, Italy; the other by the Women's Studies Centre and English Department of University College, Galway, Ireland. The Galway conference, in particular, provided the inspiration, and some of the material, for this issue: many thanks to the organizers. We will publish further articles on nationalism in the near future. Some related themes will be discussed in our forthcoming issue, on ethnicities in Britain and Europe.

Annie Whitehead
Clara Connolly
Erica Carter
Helen Crowley

WOMEN, NATIONALISM AND ISLAM IN CONTEMPORARY POLITICAL DISCOURSE IN IRAN

Nahid Yeganeh

This article aims to briefly examine the historical links between Iranian nationalism and Islam and the implications of this history for contemporary discourses on women and the family. In examining the complex evolution of Iranian political history this century, and the equally complex ways in which this has shaped women's rights and opportunities, any notion of the current discursive locations of women being a unitary effect of Islam is rejected. It will be argued that the histories of nationalism in Iran have had both particular significance and contradictory effects for women.

Women, nationalism and Islam in twentieth-century Iran

Twentieth-century transformations in the status and position of Iranian women have been closely linked with Iran's changing relation with the West. In the nineteenth century, Russian territorial intrusions in Iran resulted in the annexation of several northern provinces. The commercial and political concessions gained by the Russians fuelled rivalry with the British over trade and territory and throughout the nineteenth and twentieth century Britain, too, succeeded in signing advantageous political and commercial treaties with the rulers of the Qajar dynasty in Iran (1779–1925). The military and political superiority of Russia and Britain, and the state's capitulation to these foreign powers became a significant cause for concern amongst various sections of Iranian society (Keddie, 1981). Successive Qajar regimes responded to Western aggression with complacency and weakness and their inability to protect Iran's interest resulted in the development of an oppositional movement against the state. This movement articulated its diverse objectives in the demand for a constitution in Iran to limit the incompetence and excesses of the Qajar monarchs and bring about parliamentary rule and democracy (Abrahamian, 1982). The constitutional movement represented an alliance of influential urban groups including the Shii clergy, the business community and the secular intelligentsia. The movement also had the support of both men and women in the popular classes (Bayat-Philip, 1978). The role of the clergy within the alliance was important because of their institutional base within Iranian society. Since the sixteenth century Shiism has been the dominant branch of Islam and although it was also the state religion, historically Shiism maintained its autonomy. The Shii clergy have in consequence enjoyed an independent following amongst the population (Momen, 1985).

The constitutional movement resulted in the Constitutional Revolution of 1906–11 and the establishment of a constitutional monarchy; it created a vision of Iran as a modern society capable of challenging Western intrusion and manipulation. In addition the movement provided a unique opportunity for women to gain political experience, particularly through the emergent women's movement which was supported by the constitutionalists (Bamdad, 1977). Releasing women from bondage was seen as an important element in the strategy to modernize Iran through social and political reform. Despite varying degrees of clerical opposition to women's emancipation, and an absence of any real consensus concerning the precise nature and extent of these reforms, the constitutional movement did articulate a conceptual link between national independence and progress on the one hand, and women's emancipation on the other.

Throughout the twentieth century, nationalism provided the context in which women's position was seen as an important social issue. Iranian political discourses, whether secular or Islamic, have since regarded women as central to the future of the nation because of their role as biological reproducers, educators of children, transmitters of culture, and participants in national life. All three states which have assumed power in Iran since the dissolution of the Qajar dynasty in 1925, that is the states established by Reza Shah Pahlavi, Mohammad Reza Shah Pahlavi and the Islamic Republic, linked women's social and familial position to the status of the nation and placed gender policies at the heart of their programmes for national development and independence.

The first post-constitutional nationalist state established by Reza Shah Pahlavi (1925–41), set out to transform Iran from a dependent, backward society to a modern independent nation-state (Abrahamian, 1978). This resulted in a number of developments with immediate and long-term consequences for women. Central to these was, of course, the emergence of the state itself as an instrument of social reform. The state assumed responsibility for the health, welfare and education of the population, adopting a forceful and centralist approach to policy implementation. A state-sponsored women's organization was set up to lead the way on women's emancipation, a development which ended an era of women's independent activities (Najmabadi, 1991). The reforms introduced by Reza Shah included measures such as unveiling, provision of free education, and the opening up of employment opportunities for women. These reforms had been the goal of women activists since the turn of the century. The ambition of the state, however, in instituting these changes was to achieve national progress through the legal construction of women as social participants, educated mothers and subservient wives. The latter was regarded to be a matter of national honour and duplicated the sentiment which had insisted on a women's movement subservient to the state.

The state's policy on women's social participation did however entail meaningful change which was secured despite tremendous opposition by the Shii establishment. Family policy by contrast lacked such commitment, and 'modernization' of the family was limited to the codification of traditional Shii precepts on women's status. The Civil Code of 1936 endorsed polygamy, gave the right of divorce and custody to men, prohibited women from travelling or entering into education and employment without their husband's permission and so on. By simply codifying the prevalent and religiously supported patriarchal relations, the family laws of the 1930s strengthened the clergy's hold over the family.

By the end of Reza Shah's reign, most of the secular and Islamic forces which had been co-opted by the state had come to oppose the repression and unconstitutional methods which had become the vehicle of the Shah's modernizing policies. This opposition, which included the now disaffected women's movement, once again rallied around the demand for constitutional rule in Iran (Keddie, 1981). Despite the nationalist overtones of the Reza Shah regime, his modernization policies had resulted neither in meaningful economic change, nor political independence.

After the abdication of Reza Shah, the second Pahlavi state established by his son Mohammad Reza Shah (1941–79) continued the same pattern of political repression, social modernization, and capitulation to Western interference. Western intervention in Iran's internal affairs reached its height in the 1940s and 1950s. The Allied forces instigated the abdication of Reza Shah in 1941 because of his Nazi sympathies and put his tame son (hereafter the Shah) in his place. Furthermore, in the 1950s, Britain and the United States panicked about the Shah's failure to stop political power being transferred to the only constitutionalist Prime Minister in Iran since the Constitutional Revolution, that is Mohammad Mosaddeq, and jointly activated a *coup d'état* against *him*. During these decades Iran was also divided into zones of influence by the British and United States forces. After the fall of Mosaddeq, who was the leader of a popular liberal nationalist party and who had championed the cause of nationalizing oil, the unconstitutional rule of the Shah was consolidated and the British and American governments continued to benefit from the modernization policies of his state (Keddie, 1981).

During the 1940s and 1950s the women's movement had resumed its independent activity. Thereafter, however, it was again co-opted. The modernization of women's legal status also resumed (Sanasarian, 1982). Such changes as did occur though were fuelled as much by women's own determination as by state policies. The campaign for the vote eventually bore fruit in 1963 when, for the first time, women were fully enfranchised. The state's policies on education and employment improved the relative position of women but did little to affect the balance of power between women and men. On the one hand, the overall proportion of women entering education and employment increased: in 1976 the rate of literacy was 35.7 per cent, and 11.3 per cent of urban women had entered the work force (Beck and Keddie, 1978). In the seventies, women had participated in all levels of education and entered most of the professions, albeit often only in token numbers. On the other hand, the pattern of inequality persisted. Female literacy compared with a male rate of 74.7 per cent in 1976, and their low rate of economic activity contrasted with a participation rate of almost 90 per cent for men. Women's opportunities to enter into higher education were also much more limited than men's: in 1976 women constituted only 30 per cent of students in higher education. Moreover, women were encouraged by state policies to take up so-called feminine professions and faced discrimination and lower pay when they attempted to enter traditionally male-dominated professions. There was also a marked absence of women from top decision-making jobs. As a result of the state failure to effectively challenge the patterns of male-female inequality, modernization failed to bring about women's full integration into the process of national development (Women's Organization of Iran, 1975; Statistical Centre of Iran, 1976, 1980).

With regard to the family, women's demands eventually led to a review of family law. The Family Protection Law of 1967 and 1975 aimed to curb the excesses of male power in the family through creation of a family protection court (Beck and Keddie, 1978). Divorce and custody were brought into the jurisdiction of the courts and the grounds on which women could initiate divorce were somewhat extended; polygamy was addressed by requiring the husband to apply to the court for permission to take a second wife and have the consent of his first wife; and the minimum age of marriage was raised to twenty for men and eighteen for women (Fathi, 1985). Abortion was also legalized in certain circumstances. The improvements brought about by these reforms, however, remained limited. The Family Protection Law continued to construct women as male property. Familial changes under the Pahlavis only scratched the surface of the problem of male-female inequality and the law concentrated on curbing the excesses of male power in the family rather than fundamentally shifting it. Pahlavi gender policy did not aim to remove patriarchal relations, simply to modernize them.

The response of political forces to the Shah's repressive rule and modernization measures was twofold. While some oppositional forces, both secular and Islamic, became co-opted by the system, others became highly alienated from the state. Shiism had undergone a series of transformations in relation to its place within the Iranian political system, and its agenda on gender had been revised in interaction with other political forces (Akhavi, 1980). As the demand for a constitutional state lost its meaning when confronted with the powerful autocratic state supported by the United States, it gradually gave way to a demand for the overthrow of the Pahlavi dynasty (Fischer, 1980). Since the state had made a claim to women's liberation and the secular opposition had not constructed an alternative gender policy to that of the state, the gender aspect of the demand for the overthrow of the Pahlavi state became the preserve of the Islamic opposition.

The rise of Shiism as a popular political force in the 1970s included an appeal to women to reject 'Westernization'. The exploitation of women as 'sex objects' was identified as a product of Iran's economic and cultural dependence on the West. Women were urged to embrace the new Shii model of womanhood which represented 'authenticity' and 'independence', and emphasized women's double role as mothers and revolutionaries (Najmabadi, 1987). The radical demand for the overthrow of the Pahlavi regime and its gender policies found credence with both religious and secular women because it promised political freedom, economic equality, social justice, cultural integrity and personal fulfilment. It resulted in massive participation of women in the Iranian Revolution of 1979 which brought about the overthrow of the Pahlavi dynasty and the establishment of the Islamic Republic (Nashat, 1983).

The 1979 Revolution was the second attempt this century to redefine and change the existing relation between the state and the West, with the aim of establishing independence and democracy in Iran. But while the first attempt, the Constitutional Revolution of 1906–11, was based on the demand for political and economic independence and aimed to achieve this through emulation of Western models of modernity, the emphasis in the recent revolution was on achieving cultural independence through construction of an 'indigenous' and 'authentic' Islamic model of modernity and progress in Iran. Moreover, while the flavour of the first revolutionary discourse was liberal nationalism, the second revolutionary movement placed its trust in cultural nationalism. The adoption of Islamic ideology by the revolutionary leadership was very much linked to the question of Iran's relation with the West and its internal manifestations. The role of Shii modernism and radicalism in revolutionary mobilization was an essential one. By problematizing cultural imperialism, a new 'revolutionary' and 'authentic' Muslim culture was constructed which appealed to wide sectors of the urban population.

In this context, far from returning to traditional Islam, the Iranian Revolution of 1979 represented both historical continuity in revisiting the political demands of twentieth-century Iran, and historical

Iranian Women in anti-colonial movement of nationalisation of Iranian oil

specificity in creating a new alliance between Islam and nationalism which became the cornerstone of the Islamic Republic's gender policies.

Women and anti-imperialism in the discourse of the Islamic Republic

The Revolution of 1979 went through two years of transitional upheaval in which a variety of Islamic, nationalist and left political forces competed for state power. This power struggle was a violent one and it finally resulted in 1981 in the complete supremacy of Ayatollah Khomeini's hardline Shiism and total suppression of internal opposition by the Islamic state (Bakhash, 1984; Millet, 1982).

The Constitution of the Islamic Republic was a product of this process of power struggle and political suppression (Algar, 1980). It gave a prominent place to women, defining them as both mothers and citizens, and regarded the establishment of an Islamic nation as dependent on the Islamization of women's position. The Constitution constructed the ideal Islamic woman in opposition to Western values of womanhood. It advocated a set of patriarchal relations which strength-ened male control over women in the family while granting women the right to be active participants in society. It claimed that the new Islamic society would value women as the upholders of the family and the nation and give them the right to fulfil their natural instincts as well as participate in social life.

However, the Islamic alternative on the position of women proposed by the Constitution in opposition to 'alien Western concepts' was far from a pure Islamic construct. On the contrary, the Constitution borrowed from a variety of indigenous and exogenous models of womanhood and reflected a compromise between conflicting sets of ideas. Indeed, it was the context of revolutionary populism and anti-imperialism which determined which concepts and ideas on women found their way into the Constitution as 'Islamic' and which ones were excluded as 'un-Islamic'. The result was a total reversal of the history of clerical opposition to women's participation in society. The same clerics who had in the 1960s objected to women's enfranchisement on religious grounds were, in the 1980s, prepared to grant women the right to vote in the name of Islam.

After the consolidation of state power by Islamic hardliners and the establishment of the discourse of Islamization, the state set out to implement the constitutional gender relations and actualize the ideal Islamic family proposed in it. This was, however, set against the context of Islamic diversity, power struggles, political repression, ideological control, economic stagnation, war and destruction, and international isolation (Milani, 1988). The gender policy of the Islamic state was not a straight replica of the Qoran, the shariat or any other ready-made Islamic gender policy. On the contrary, it was the result of a number of concrete factors and processes.

First, the discourse of Islamization was constructed as events developed in the post-revolutionary society. Historical conceptions of gender were drawn upon in the process of encoding the immediate social and political situation. Second, the discourse of Islamization did not develop in a unified manner. Although its framework was set in opposition to the Pahlavi system and related 'alien Western concepts of gender', nevertheless the Islamization policy was formulated in a heterogeneous and *ad hoc* manner by a variety of sources with different and sometimes conflicting interests. Political debate and power struggles between various Islamic factions led to the dominance of some Islamization concepts as opposed to others. Third, the discourse of Islamization faced a serious crisis not only in relation to policy formulation but also in relation to implementation. Political repression, power struggles and economic stagnation affected the ability of the state to set coherent policies and ensure their effective implementation. As a result of all this, what was or was not accepted as Islamic in relation to gender was determined by the post-revolutionary power relation, the radical political culture, and the economic realities of the time.

The Islamic Republic's gender policies were developed and implemented within the above social context. The actualization of Islamic family and nation involved extensive Islamization of women (Tabari

Rural women workers

and Yeganeh, 1982). Initially this required a codification of the 'Islamic family'. Policies were developed on marriage, family planning, familial relations, divorce and custody to Islamize and standardize the Iranian household (Fathi, 1985; Haeri, 1989). Related to this process was establishing the degree of women's participation in national development. Policies were formulated on women's education, employment and political participation to ensure that the Islamic nation continued to benefit from the creative and nurturing qualities of its female citizens. The third aspect of the Islamic gender relations concerned formation of strategies to enable the family and the nation to remain in harmony in relation to women. Policies were developed on gender segregation and punishment of adultery to de-sexualize male-female social contact and hence protect the sanctity of the Islamic family (Afshar, 1988; Najmabadi, 1991).

Family
Islamization of women's position started with Ayatollah Khomeini's prompt abolition of the family courts and the Family Protection Law. This effectively returned women's legal status within the family to the family laws of the 1930s which were regarded by Ayatollah Khomeini as proper and Islamic. The family-planning policies of the Pahlavi regime

were also abandoned, abortion was made illegal, and large families were encouraged. However, despite its initial abrogation of Pahlavi family laws, the Islamic Republic gradually began to move towards reinstating them (*Zan-e Rooz, Ettelaat, Keyhan Havai*, 1979–89). This shift arose from at least two sources of opposition.

The first of these was that of the moderate lobby, which included the Islamic women's movement, as well as different ruling factions powerful at different stages of the Islamic Republic. As a result of this lobby, the family court, known as the special civil court, was revived and mandated to deal with divorce. However, male authority was preserved by allowing the husband to register divorce without court permission if the wife consented. This was a compromise solution so that the concept of family court could be retained despite the theoretical removal of the Family Protection Law from the statute books. Since 1979, consistent lobbying has taken place by the Islamic women's movement with the backing of the moderate factions of the state to improve the balance of power between the family court and the male head of the family to the advantage of the court (*Zan-e Rooz, Ettelaat, Keyhan Havai*, 1979–89).

The second source of opposition arose out of the diversity of Shii jurisprudence and the existence of multiple centres of power in the Islamic Republic. In Shii Islam, high-ranking clerics (known as *mojta-hedin*) have the right to issue independent verdicts on all aspects of life based on their own interpretations of Shii law. As a result of this tradition, judicial topics attracted a number of different Shii interpretations despite the efforts of the state to standardize the family law. For example, two differing opinions were expressed on the issue of polygamy. While the Council of Guardians considered polygamy a man's unconditional right, those who administered the law, that is the special civil courts, followed the practice of obtaining the first wife's permission for legitimate polygamy.

This meant that despite its abrogation, parts of the Family Protection Law were still in force. In fact, in 1989, an authoritative collection of the Islamic Republic's family laws brought together a number of valid sources of legal guidance on the family. These included the Civil Code of 1936, the Family Protection Law (1967 and 1975), the Special Civil Courts Act 1979, other related legislation passed by the parliaments and the Council of Guardians, regulations and opinions issued by the High Council of Judiciary and General Board of Supreme Court, and various verdicts by Ayatollah Khomeini (Ghorbani, 1989).

Social participation
The second aspect of the Islamization of women's position concerned women's participation in national development. The Islamic Republic formulated a series of policies on women's social participation, including in politics, education and employment.

Contrary to expectations by secular forces, the Islamic state did not prevent women from engaging in education. Indeed, women's education was considered as an important strategy for the Islamization of society.

This was because the role played by women in linking the home and the school was considered crucial. Furthermore, women's presence in educational institutions was a political urgency. The Islamic state had to fill the schools and universities with its female supporters to counteract the influence of the secular middle classes. In a country with a young and politically active population, the education system was an important site of ideological struggle and the Islamic state was determined to take over and control it by replacing secular students with religious ones.

During its first decade, the Islamic Republic did not pose any obstacles to women's professional training. Training for favoured professions, such as teaching, nursing and midwifery, was encouraged at all levels from schools to university. The most rapidly expanding area of women's education was Islamic theology. However, the Islamic Republic's attempt to establish Islamic gender relations in education did affect women adversely. Islamization was achieved through gender segregation in the education system, imposition of *hejab* (Islamic clothing) on women, reinforcement of gender division of subjects, and preservation of male dominance in education. Women's education, although highly encouraged in official pronouncements, suffered in reality due to such Islamization measures combined with lack of co-ordination between multiple centres of decision-making and lack of financial resources arising from economic stagnation (*Zan-e Rooz, Ettelaat, Keyhan Havai*, 1979–89).

With regard to women's higher education, the policy adopted by the Islamic Republic proved contradictory and controversial, and as a result had to be amended a number of times. Before the Revolution, women were admitted to all fields of study except mining. During the transitional period, women's entry to higher education remained as before. The 'cultural revolution' which resulted in the Islamization of the higher education system during the politically extremist period of 1980–4, entailed a most restrictive policy towards women's entry to 'non-feminine' fields. Women's entry to a whole range of technical, engineering and experimental sciences was prohibited (Ghahreman, 1988).

Moreover, restrictions were imposed on women's admission to most medical, environmental and human sciences by specifying a maximum number of places for women which ranged from 20 to 50 per cent. Women who were attending the prohibited courses were asked to either drop out or change subject. On the whole, slightly over half of all subjects offered within higher education were closed to women (Mojab, 1991). But the gender division of subjects also affected men who were prohibited from entering subjects such as midwifery, family hygiene and sewing. Men were admitted for nursing but were allocated a maximum admission quota of 50 per cent. (Ghahreman, 1988) However, despite these limitations, the number of women in higher education in the 1980s increased compared with the 1970s. Furthermore, as a result of various pressures, the subject restrictions for women were gradually eased and in 1989 they were removed altogether (Ghahreman, 1988).

A related field of interest for the Islamic state was women's employment. Here, too, the Islamic regime adopted a strict stance against Pahlavi policies in formulating their 'Islamic' alternative. No other aspect of women's social involvement, however, presented such problems for the Islamic Republic's policy-makers as did women's employment. The difficulty presented by women's economic activity arose out of the conflicting economic, political and ideological imperatives faced by the Islamic state.

The early post-revolutionary years witnessed a number of attacks on women's employment. Women were barred from becoming judges immediately after the revolution. The next step was to cleanse the workplace and the first and foremost target was the public sector where the intelligentsia of the Pahlavi era had spread roots. Ayatollah Khomeini's call in the summer of 1980 for an 'Administrative Revolution' started the cleansing operation which included the imposition of *hejab* on women employees, segregation of male and female workers, silencing or sacking of non-Islamic employees, replacing secular employees in key posts with Islamic sympathizers, and installing Islamic societies in all state organizations as instruments of control and Islamization. Women employees were particularly vulnerable in this process and large numbers of women were sacked for protesting against the forceful imposition of *hejab* or left voluntarily to avoid wearing *hejab*. However, once the transitional period was over and the Islamic regime felt politically secure, the emphasis of the state policy began to change from an *ad hoc* replacement of Pahlavi practices to that of formulating a more systematic policy on women's employment. The main elements of the new policy included an emphasis on the ideological importance of training women for certain professions such as education, welfare, health and medicine, and the adaptation of women's employment to the needs of the 'Islamic family' (*Zan-e Rooz, Ettelaat, Keyhan Havai*, 1979–89)

The Islamic Republic's policies towards women's employment did not reverse the rising trend of female employment in Iran. Women's employment both in the formal and non-formal sectors, but particularly in the latter, expanded mainly due to economic needs. Statistics show that the number of economically active urban women in the formal sector increased from 11.3 per cent in 1976 to 12.6 per cent in 1982 (Moghadam, 1988; Statistical Centre of Iran, 1980–90). However, contradictory policies, mismanagement of the economy, imposition of gender restrictions, and encouragement of male domination all acted to reduce the overall opportunities open to women in education and employment during the first decade of the Islamic Republic.

Women's participation in politics legitimized the state's Islamic policies and created an image of popular support and stability internally and internationally. Ayatollah Khomeini considered women's participation in the anti-Shah Revolution crucial in saving Islam from 'captivity by foreigners' (*Zan-e Rooz, Ettelaat, Keyhan Havai*, 1979–89). After the revolution, various factions of the state and revolutionary grass-roots organizations attempted to harness women's tremendous mobilization potential (Tabari and Yeganeh, 1982). The hardline faction of the state took control of women's mass mobilization by organizing mass rallies in support of the state's Islamization policies and against the demands of both secular and Islamic opposition. Oppositional demonstrations and rallies often faced women's counter-demonstrations in support of the hardline faction of the state. Women's mass support was also manipulated in relation to two other areas of importance to the survival of the state, those of the election and the war with Iraq. Women's electoral participation was of prime importance for the Islamic Republic's populist image. This was specially so in a context in which people were asked to cast votes in eleven parliamentary and presidential elections in the first decade of the Islamic Republic (Tabari and Yeganeh, 1982).

Women's participation in the Iran-Iraq war was also encouraged by the state. Ayatollah Khomeini made several rousing speeches to promote women's strategic importance (Tabari and Yeganeh, 1982). Women's role was multifaceted. Initially, they were expected to provide ideological support, but as the war progressed and the possibility of an early settlement of the conflict with Iraq receded, a much more pragmatic and systematic approach was taken towards women's involvement. Women were recruited as revolutionary guards and mobilized for military action. Despite his earlier statement that Islam does not allow women's participation in a holy war (*jihad*), Ayatollah Khomeini instructed women to take up military training in the name of Islam to defend their country (Tabari and Yeganeh, 1982).

While women from the lower classes provided the mass support that the Islamic regime needed, Islamic women leaders engaged in the women's movement. Despite their relative success in pressurizing for improvements in Islamic rights for women, Islamic women leaders were on the whole presented with limited opportunity to enter into top decision-making, and struggled to find a role for themselves in the higher echelons of the Islamic society. Islamic women activists were largely engaged in philanthropic and religious activities and only a handful made it to the Islamic Parliament (*Majlis*) and government. Eleven elections during the first decade of the Islamic Republic produced 6 women *Majlis* representatives in all. This was even more tokenistic than in the Shah's regime, where in the last Pahlavi *Majlis* and Senate, out of 270 members only 18 were women and only one woman was a Minister.

Individual rights
The third aspect of the Islamization of women's position after the revolution was individual and human rights. Ayatollah Motahhari, one of the ideologues of the Islamic protest movement in Iran in the 1970s, rejected the concept of 'individual rights' as a Western irrelevance. He believed that Islam prioritized the right of the Muslim community over the right of the individual. In his view, the interest of the Muslim

community in defining women's appearance and sexuality takes precedence over women's individual choice (Motahhari, 1978). This view became the official policy in the Islamic Republic. If women were to have a presence outside the home, they had to be de-sexualized to protect the Islamic nation from corruption. The Islamic Republic had to devise various strategies to protect the society from the side-effects of women's social participation. Two of these strategies were *hejab* and punishment of adultery.

Hejab and other forms of gender segregation were deeply rooted traditions in Iran, but they were considered to be the hallmarks of backwardness. The Pahlavi era had by no means succeeded in totally eradicating these practices. Pre-revolutionary Iranian society had remained quite conservative in relation to male-female integration. Before the revolution, the mainstream education system was segregated except for some private schools and the universities. Although men and women could mix freely at work and in the public domain, nevertheless women were restricted by acceptable codes of behaviour, dress and speech. In short, gender segregation and *hejab* were not new concepts introduced to Iranian society by the Islamic regime. Using force to regulate women's clothing, too, was not a new phenomenon. Reza Shah's forcible removal of women's *hejab* in the 1930s was part of the contemporary history of gender relations. But the new development in the post-revolutionary situation was the Islamic Republic's reversal of the twentieth-century trend of gender desegregation. *Hejab* and public segregation of men and women were for the first time being constructed by the state as a superior form of gender relation and a signifier of Islamic modernity. The Islamic state's enforcement of *hejab* and male-female segregation was giving these traditional practices a new political dimension. Their purpose was the protection of the Islamic family.

The process of the imposition of *hejab* was a long and difficult one and it has become one of the most fiercely implemented policies of the Islamic Republic. The full imposition of *hejab* and sex segregation, however, is yet to be achieved by the Islamic state (*Zan-e Rooz, Ettelaat, Keyhan Havai*, 1979–89). Even though the Islamic uniform has been fully imposed on women, individual taste and pursuit of fashion have not been completely eradicated. Women forced into segregation and *hejab* use every opportunity to defy it. Men and women are still appearing in public together. Many women mock their imposed *hejab* by showing strings of hair or leaving traces of make-up on their faces (Najmabadi, 1991). Moreover, the state policy on *hejab* and the forceful method of its imposition have also been opposed by moderate sections of the Islamic women's movement. The Islamic Republic's policy on women's *hejab* and desegregation in its first decade ended as it began with divided opinions, disillusionment and resistance.

Another systematic violation of women's individual rights took place through anti-corruption policies. While *hejab* and sex segregation were familiar concepts for Iranians, the Islamic Republic's anti-corruption measures as a legitimate method of policing the family were somewhat novel concepts within the twentieth-century Iranian political discourses. The definition of corruption was extended by the state to cover adultery, homosexuality, drug abuse, alcohol consumption as well as a whole range of social and cultural activities such as gambling, entertainment, music, any type of mixing of men and women and wearing of un-Islamic clothes by women (*Zan-e Rooz, Ettelaat, Keyhan Havai*, 1979–89). The state set up a Bureau For Combatting Corruption to cleanse the post-revolutionary society of the manifestation of 'Westernized' gender relations and put an end to 'free relationships' between men and women. The most drastic measure taken by the Islamic state to protect the Islamic family was pronouncing sex outside marriage an offence punishable by death. Adultery and homosexuality had always been considered punishable offences in Iranian law, but their punishment assumed new dimensions in the Islamic Republic and as the family turned into a more overt political institution the violation of its sanctity became a political crime requiring punishments such as execution, stoning, flogging, exile and shaving of hair.

The anti-corruption campaign aimed to guard the Islamic family against the evil of illegitimate sex. The result of the Islamic discourse of sex, sin and violence was a horrifying atmosphere of state and domestic violence against women which has claimed the lives of many female victims and made a lasting impact on gender relations in Iran (*Zan-e Rooz, Ettelaat, Keyhan Havai*, 1979–89).

Concluding remarks

In the first decade of its existence the elaboration of the gender policies of the Islamic Republic was greatly influenced by the political and economic circumstances faced by the post-revolutionary society. As with other political discourses in twentieth-century Iran, the link between nationalism and Islam was crucial in determining the gender policies of the Islamic Republic. The development of Islamic nationalism in the 1970s as a revolutionary discourse facilitated the emergence of the Islamic Republic. After the consolidation of the Islamic Republic into an Islamic theocracy, nationalism as a mobilizing force was politically marginalized. The state achieved this marginalization by representing nationalism as synonymous with anti-imperialism on the one hand, and replacing nationalism with Islam as the main mass mobilization force, on the other. The new alliance between Islam and anti-imperialism constituted the cornerstone of the Islamization policies of the state. The context of revolutionary populism, anti-imperialism and internal power struggles determined which concepts and ideas on women were defined as 'Islamic' and which as 'un-Islamic'.

This resulted in a particular combination of positive and negative policies on women. The discourse of Islamization on the one hand did not exclude women from participation in society as women remained active in the social sphere and participated in even greater numbers in educational, welfare, economic and political activities. But on the other hand, the state's enforced Islamization attempted to engineer a particular gender division of labour in the family and society which affected women's opportunities negatively. Furthermore, women were promised the fulfilment of their 'natural' rights and roles. Woman as wife, mother and citizen was offered a bargain with the state. Women were to receive economic and legal protection by the Islamic state and its representative at home, that is the male head of the family. In return, they had to prove their credentials as obedient wives, self-sacrificing mothers and active citizens (Kandiyoti, 1992). In reality, however, this bargain did not work: male domination in the family was strengthened by Islamization, and women's familial rights diminished leading to a significant deterioration of the living conditions of women. The Islamic Republic may have given its female supporters the opportunity for popular political participation and a sense of righteousness and self-worth. But it seriously undermined their position within the family and violated their individual and human rights.

Notes

Nahid Yeganeh has completed her Ph.D at the University of London and works in the field of women and development. This article is based on her doctoral thesis, *Women in Political Discourses of Twentieth-century Iran*, which is to be published by Cambridge University Press.

References

ABRAHAMIAN, Ervand (1982) *Iran Between Two Revolutions* Princeton: Princeton University Press.

AFSHAR, Haleh (1988) 'Behind the veil: the public and private faces of Khomeini's policies on Iranian women' in AGARWAL, Bina (1988) editor, *Structures of Patriarchy: the State, the Community and the Household* London: Zed Books.

AKHAVI, Shahrough (1980) *Religion and Politics in Contemporary Iran: Clergy-State Relations in the Pahlavi Period* Albany: State University of New York Press.

ALGAR, Hamid (1980) *The Constitution of the Islamic Republic* (translation) Berkley: Mizan Press.

BAKHASH, Shaul (1984) *The Reign of the Ayatollahs: Iran and the Islamic Revolution* New York: Basic Books.

BAMDAD, Badr ol-moluk (1977) *From Darkness into Light: Women's Emancipation in Iran* (edited and translated by F. R. C. Bagley) New York: Exposition Press.

BAYAT-PHILIP, Mangol (1978) 'Women and revolution in Iran' in BECK and KEDDIE (1978).

BECK, Louise and KEDDIE, Nikki (1978) editors, *Women in the Muslim World* Cambridge: Harvard University Press.

ETTELAAT (1979–89) daily newspaper.

FATHI, Asghar (1985) *Women and the Family in Iran* Leiden: J. Brill.

FISCHER, Michael (1980) *Iran: From Religious Dispute to Revolution* Cambridge: Harvard University Press.

GHAHREMAN, Sahar (1988) 'The Islamic state's policy towards women's access to higher education and its socio-economic effects' *Nimeye Digar: Iranian Women's Feminist Journal* No. 7.

GHORBANI, Farajollah (1989) *Family: the Complete Collection of Laws and Regulations* Tehran: Tus Publishers.

HAERI, Shahla (1989) *The Law of Desire* London: I. B. Tauris.

KANDIYOTI, Deniz (1992) 'Islam and patriarchy: a comparative perspective' in KEDDIE, Nikki and BARON, Beth (1992) *Women in Middle Eastern History* New Haven and London: Yale University Press.

KEDDIE, Nikki (1981) *Roots of Revolution* New Haven and London: Yale University Press.

KEYHAN HAVAI (1979–89) weekly edition of a daily newspaper.

MILANI, Mohsen (1988) *The Making of Iran's Islamic Revolution: From Monarchy to Islamic Republic* Boulder: Westview Press.

MILLET, Kate (1982) *Going to Iran* New York: Coward, McCann & Geoghegan.

MOGHADAM, Valentine (1988) 'Women, work and ideology in the Islamic Republic' *International School of Middle East Studies* Vol 20.

MOJAB, Shahrzad (1991) 'State control and women's resistance in Iranian universities' *Nimeye Digar: Iranian Women's Feminist Journal* No. 14.

MOMEN, Moojan (1985) *An Introduction to Shii Islam* New Haven and London: Yale University Press.

MOTAHHARI, Morteza (1978) *The System of Women's Rights in Islam*. Tehran.

NAJMABADI, Afsaneh (1987) 'Iran's turn to Islam: from modernism to a moral order' *Middle East Journal* Vol. 4, No. 20.

—— (1991) in KANDIYOTI, Deniz (1991) *Women, Islam and State* London: Macmillan Press.

NASHAT, Guity (1983) editor, *Women and Revolution in Iran* Boulder: Westview Press.

SANASARIAN, Eliz (1982) *The Women's Rights Movement in Iran* New York: Praeger.

STATISTICAL CENTRE OF IRAN (1976, 1980–90) *Statistical Yearbook of Iran* Tehran: Plan and Budget Organization.

TABARI, Azar and YEGANEH, Nahid (1982) *In the Shadow of Islam: Women's Movement in Iran* London: Zed Books.

WOMEN'S ORGANIZATION OF IRAN (1975) *The Employment of Women* Tehran: Women's Organization of Iran.

ZAN-E ROOZ (1979–89) women's weekly magazine.

FEMINISM, CITIZENSHIP AND NATIONAL IDENTITY

Ann Curthoys

Australia must work through its identity crisis. It is an Asian nation with a European heritage. (Race Discrimination Commissioner, Irene Moss, 26 January 1992)

More than 200 years ago, the British King claimed land rights to about two thirds of the countries of this continent, an area the size of Western Europe, by setting up camp on the eastern shore on January 26, 1788. . . . There is only *one way* Australians can belong here. This is not part of Asia, Race Discrimination Commissioner Irene Moss needs to understand this. Your continuing failure over the past 200 years to treat with us as equals will condemn you, all of you, as a community of thieves in the eyes of your children's children, and the rest of the world. We are your only true connection to this continent, to this entire region. We are the land, and we are here forever. (Aboriginal community leader Shirley Smith (Mum Shirl), 28 January 1992)[1]

I tell you I learnt one thing: I learnt about self-respect and self-regard for Australia. Not about some cultural cringe to a country which decided not to defend the Malaysian peninsular, not to worry about Singapore, not to give us our troops back to keep ourselves free from Japanese domination. This was the country you people wedded yourselves to, and even when they walked out on you and joined the Common Market you were still looking for your MBEs and your knighthoods and all the rest of the regalia that comes with it. These are the same old fogies who doffed their lids and tugged the forelock to the British establishment. We will not have a bar of it. (Australian Prime Minister, Paul Keating, speech attacking his Liberal and National Party opponents in the House of Representatives, 24 February 1992)[2]

> We took the traditional lands and smashed the traditional way of life. We
> brought the diseases and the alcohol. We committed the murders. We took
> the children from their mothers. We practised discrimination and
> exclusion. It was our ignorance and our prejudice – and our failure to
> imagine these things being done to us. . . . We failed to see what we were
> doing degraded us all. . . . Imagine if ours was the oldest culture in the
> world and we were told that it was worthless. Imagine if we had resisted
> this settlement, suffered and died in the defence of our land, and then
> were told in history books that we'd given up without a fight. Imagine if
> non-Aboriginal Australians had served their country in peace and war
> and were then ignored in history books. (Australian Prime Minister, Paul
> Keating, on the occasion of the launching of the 1993 International Year
> for the World's Indigenous People, 10 December 1992)

Strange things are happening in Australia in the early 1990s, the
beginning of an unpredictable *fin de siècle*. As the fifty-year echo of
certain key events in the Second World War reverberated through our
lives, history was mobilized throughout 1992 in national public debate
to argue for particular internal and foreign policy changes: looser ties
with Britain, a stronger independent national identity expressed
symbolically through a new flag and other cultural icons, 'reconciliation'
between Aboriginal people and other Australians, and closer economic
and cultural ties with Australia's Asian neighbours. As the rest of the
world continues to fall more clearly into geographically defined trading
and economic blocs, leaving Australia in danger of even greater isolation
and of becoming rather more unique than many Australians would like,
the massive contradiction of modern Australian society, the gap
between geographical and cultural-historical codes of belonging in the
world, remains as sharp as ever.

The question of national identity is a subject for ongoing political
debate. Each year Australia Day, celebrated on 26 January, the
anniversary of the establishment of British rule on the Australian
continent, evokes – like all commemorations, anniversaries and
national birthdays – a certain amount of historical consciousness and
debate. In 1988, two hundred years since the first British settlement on
Australian soil, the whole year was given over to discussion of questions
of national identity. Intended officially as a celebration of British
settlement, 1988 became, in fact, an opportunity seized very effectively
by Aboriginal people to assert their claims to sovereignty on the basis of
their prior occupation, their presence, not for a mere 200 years, but for at
least 40,000 (Spearritt, 1988).

As it turned out, 1992 was even more interesting than 1988 as an
instance of the historiographical maxim that competing versions of the
past become ways of arguing for a different future. On 26 January, 1992,
there was talk, as there has been each year in the recent past, of
republicanism, the need for a new flag, the implications of multiculturalism for Australian national identity, Australian relations to
Asia, and especially of Aboriginal history and present demands.

Aboriginal land rights march

Drawing attention to Aboriginal history and demands was the celebration of the twentieth anniversary of the Tent Embassy of 1972, which had protested against the government's rejection of land-rights claims by setting up a tent on the lawns outside Parliament House and announcing it, tellingly, in a striking use of symbolic politics, as an 'embassy'. In 1992, a group of about forty Aboriginal people, including some who had been in the original protest, occupied the Old Parliament House in Canberra, again claiming it as an Aboriginal embassy (*SMH*, 28.1.92). On a somewhat different tack, Discrimination Commissioner Irene Moss, herself of Chinese descent, attracted attention when she described Australia as an Asian nation with a European heritage. (*SMH*, 27.1.92). Her remarks were attacked by a number of Aboriginal commentators, including respected community leader Shirley Smith (Mum Shirl), who wrote, in the terms quoted in the epigraph opening this essay, that it was through recognition of the indigenous Aboriginal past, not false claims of being part of Asia, that Australians might find a way of belonging.

Into this *mélange* of discussion on issues to do with identity, multiculturalism, heritage, and history came the fiftieth anniversary of key events of the Second World War: the fall of Singapore on

15 February 1942, and the Japanese bombing, four days later, of Australia's northernmost city, Darwin. This apparently historical and reflective moment came to intertwine with immediate political debates. *The Australian* commemorated the fall of Singapore with articles by historians on the reasons for it, and on the bloody retreat from Malaya and the experiences of prisoners of war. At a service to commemorate those killed during the Japanese bombing of Darwin, Prime Minister Paul Keating took the opportunity to reflect that the Pacific War demonstrated once and for all that Australia was geographically part of the Asian region (*SMH*, 25.2.92).

It was in this setting, amid hectic talk of republicanism and British wartime betrayal, that the Queen visited Sydney in late February 1992 for the sesquicentenary of its incorporation as a municipality, a visit which had seemed a public relations bonanza when planned a year or so before, but now appeared just a little risky in this decidedly jumpy and increasingly less royalist atmosphere (though, for royalists, the worst was definitely yet to come). To unbalance things even more, the Prime Minister was new, Paul Keating having gained the leadership only a couple of months earlier. Of Irish descent, his wife of Dutch origin, devastatingly sarcastic in parliament, formerly the Treasurer, an economic rationalist interested in deregulation and reduction in economic protection, Keating is a passionate nationalist and a republican.

The presence of the British Queen, also nominally Queen of Australia, stimulated rather than silenced the expression of republican sentiment. She was welcomed by the Prime Minister in Canberra with a blunt speech on the theme of Australia's continuing evolution into independence: 'Just as Great Britain some time ago sought to make her future secure in the European Community, so Australia now vigorously seeks partnerships with countries in our own region. Our outlook is necessarily independent.' (*SMH*, 25.2.92) And then, of course, he famously breached convention and protocol by placing his antipodean hand on the Queen's back during a reception, a gesture regarded as shocking by some in Australia as well as many in Britain.

When, a little later, the Queen having returned home, the conservative Opposition accused him of having no respect for her, not like the respect shown during the 1954 royal tour, Keating saw his opportunity. In a parliamentary speech, he was scathing about any desire to return to the 1950s (when the conservative parties dominated electorally), portraying it as a time of economic and cultural stagnation. He poured scorn on the conservative side of politics for its continuing attachment to an increasingly irrelevant royalty and developed his theme further in radio and television interviews, claiming that Australia's time as a 'cultural derivative of Britain' was over and finished. (*SMH*, 28.2.92) He thought most of the reaction against him overseas was coming from Fleet Street's 'low life' tabloids and conservative voices in the 'creaks and crevices of the British establishment.' (*The Australian*, 29.2.92)

Prime Minister Keating was well aware that his appeal to national identity, like all such appeals, while claiming to speak for all

Australians, risked speaking only to sections of the population. His nationalism was founded on an interestingly inclusive version of Australian history, seeking to draw the whole population, Aboriginal, British-descended, other European, and Asian, into a modern Australian self-conscious collectivity.[3] This construction of Australian national identity was grounded thoroughly in a particular version of history, based on an old Irish-Australian Catholic working-class right-wing Labor consciousness. In this narrative, the labour movement had the best chance of embodying the ideals of the country as a whole. 'Britain' signified 'the establishment' and conservatism, while 'Australia' was constructed as a contested territory of unending battle between the labour movement and conservative reaction, where the conservatives usually won. It is a portrait of Australian history and national identity which closely followed that of Australia's most famous left-wing pre-World War II historian, Brian Fitzpatrick, also of Irish origin, whose books bore titles like *British Imperialism and Australia*, *The British Empire and Australia, The Australian People* and *A Short History of the Australian Labour Movement*. Don Watson, Fitzpatrick's biographer, and, very significantly, Keating's speechwriter, portrayed in his book *Brian Fitzpatrick: A Radical Life* how Fitzpatrick loathed Australian economic, cultural and political subservience to Britain (and later, the United States). Fitzpatrick's thesis was that the economic development of the Australian colonies was tied always to British designs and interests, and underlying all his histories was a desire for a truly economically independent Australian nation. For Fitzpatrick, radical politics and Australian nationalism were two sides of the same coin, and Keating's talk of self-respect echoed and brought to new life Fitzpatrick's repeated concern with the theme of national self-respect (Watson, 1979).

Aboriginal people and the nation

Keating was very careful to address Aboriginal people in his talk of the need for an independent Australian nation. His comments changed, and became stronger, as 1992 progressed. At the service to commemorate those killed during the Japanese bombing of Darwin in February 1942, he recalled and honoured the role played by Aboriginal people in the defence of their country (*SMH*, 25.2.92). In announcing in June an extra $400 million in new assistance to Aboriginal communities as part of the government's response to the damning Report of the Royal Commission into Aboriginal Deaths in Police Custody, Keating described it as 'Australia's last chance this century to address white Australia's injustice to blacks' (*SMH*, 24.6.92).

Keating ended 1992, on the occasion of the beginning of the International Year of Indigenous Peoples, with a statement, the strongest by any political leader yet, recognizing past brutality and inhumanity towards Aboriginal people, and Aboriginal Australians as the original inhabitants of the country. The speech was direct as to where historical responsibility lay: 'It was we who did the dispossessing . . . we committed the murders . . .' His comments were immediately endorsed by the Aboriginal and Torres Strait Islander Commission and the Council for Aboriginal Reconciliation, as ushering in a new approach to Aboriginal-European relations. The significant shift was away from a model of Aboriginal inclusion, towards one where recognition of prior ownership and occupation might provide the basis for subsequent and future self-determination and sovereignty. Keating also recognized the historical importance of the Mabo decision in the High Court in June, a decision which overthrew the doctrine of *terra nullius* and established a fundamental legal recognition of indigenous prior land ownership, and therefore a 'basis for justice'.

Pathbreakingly, Keating took up the emphasis Aboriginal people themselves place on the fact of invasion itself, and their particular rights and status as the original inhabitants of the land. Aboriginal groups have increasingly insisted on a history which stresses their difference, their direct experience of invasion and racism, but also the ways in which it is their internal social relationships, their connexions with each other, that matter to them most of all. Talk of inclusion is often not welcomed. Aboriginal people continue to see non-Aboriginal Australians as British (or European, or Asian), always from somewhere else, the invasionary Other.

Multiculturalism

Keating was also concerned to address immigrants of all ethnic origins in relation to his Australian nation. Part of the basis for his republicanism, indeed, and a major reason perhaps for its appeal, is the highly diverse ethnic composition of the population, and Keating emphasized the importance of multiculturalism to Australia's future. Yet ideals of plurality and diversity rarely sit very comfortably with notions of a singular national identity. Keating in one speech suggested that multiculturalism has combined with 'the lingering Britishness of the place to circumvent the emergence of a singularly Australian identity to replace the old imperial one . . . we have to make clear that our . . . encouragement of ethnic diversity in no way compromises our expectation that the first loyalty of all who make their home here will be to Australia.' As a step in that direction he suggested that the Oath of Allegiance which immigrants seeking naturalization must take should be changed from swearing loyalty to the Queen to swearing their loyalty to Australia 'and the things we believe Australia stands for – including liberty, tolerance, social justice – those very beliefs which underpin multiculturalism' (*SMH*, 27.6.92). And as I write, the government has just announced that new Australian citizens will no longer swear allegiance to the Queen and her heirs and successors, and will instead pledge loyalty to Australia and its people (*SMH*, 18.12.92).

Feminism and the state

Where does all this talk of national identity leave the feminist project? Are not feminists true internationalists, indifferent to and critical of yearnings for national identity? In the Australian context, can women, thought of as a group cutting across ethnic lines, be included in the idea of a new Australian nation? Many second-wave feminists have traditionally thought not, regarding white Australian national identity as a masculinist enterprise, calling up a traditional figure, the itinerant outback white single male, with his ideal free, unencumbered, yet convivial lifestyle (Lake, 1986). Feminists point to the turn-of-the-century slogan – 'Australia for the White Man' – adopted by a legendary journal, *The Bulletin*, noting not only its evident racism, but also its assumption of the true Australian as inevitably and only male. National history is sometimes regarded by feminists as entirely male, and feminist history, and feminism generally, are represented, by contrast, as distinctively internationalist (Reekie, 1992).

THE NATIONAL AUSTRALIAN NEWSPAPER
"Australia for the White Man."

Keating, at any rate, is determined that feminists be self-consciously Australian. To his staff of advisers, he has added Anne Summers, author of one of Australia's best-known second-wave feminist history texts, *Damned Whores and God's Police: The Colonisation of Women in Australia* (1975), which influentially argued that the way in which Australian history, culture and society was generally conceptualized and understood was based on images of male Australians only. In a speech on 26 June 1992, Keating suggested that in the ongoing task of redefining themselves, Australians need to abandon and combat the traditional image of the Australian male. A new sense of what Australian men stood for would better reflect contemporary attitudes to women. The day before, the chair of the United Nations Committee on the Elimination of Discrimination against Women had suggested to him that Australian legislation was a model for the rest of the world. 'Nowhere,' said Keating, 'in the image we present to the rest of the world – nor I suspect in our self-image – is there a reflection of that fact.' Australians, Keating argues, should be proud of feminist advances, and its legislation guaranteeing equal rights for women.

It is not only Keating who has emphasized Australian feminism's legislative successes. Many observers, from within and without, have remarked on this one outstanding feature of Australian feminism: its close interaction with the nation-state as a means of achieving its ends, much closer than in two otherwise very comparable societies, the USA and Great Britain. This significant engagement with the state has meant not only fighting politically for appropriate reform legislation, but also direct involvement in state bureaucracies. A specifically Australian term – 'femocrats' – has been coined to describe feminists who have entered the state bureaucracy to achieve feminist ends.

The Women's Liberation movement, when it came to prominence in early 1970, did not initially seek to influence the state from within. Based on a far-left socialist tradition, its prevailing philosophy and rhetoric was revolutionary, its ideas and organizational skills honed in the anti-Vietnam War movement. Early women's liberation theory was initially shaped by Marxism, but quickly developed some rather non-Marxist characteristics. A Marxist interest in the value of women's labour was combined with an argument that women as a group were oppressed on the basis of sexist ideology. There was a tension within such Women's Liberation theory between an awareness – derived from the Marxist and New Left influence in the movement – of the class (and to some extent ethnic) differences between women, and a feminist assertion of their unity in oppression. The new movement saw direct forms of public protest, seeking to influence the state from *without*, as appropriate forms of political activity. A major political campaign was for women's right of access to safe and cheap abortion. The main aim was to change consciousness. Party and parliamentary politics were not, for most, an appropriate or effective option.

Within two years of the establishment of Women's Liberation in Australia, however, the first serious inroad into parliamentary politics was made with the establishment of the Women's Electoral Lobby (WEL), which through its participation in the Federal election campaign in 1972, placed feminist demands on the wider political agenda. WEL grew directly from Women's Liberation groups in Victoria, but quickly developed a far more direct emphasis on attempting to achieve change through pressure on the existing political parties. It was able to place pressure most successfully on the Australian Labor Party, and seems to have assisted its success. The Whitlam Labor Government was elected in December 1972 for all sorts of reasons, but it was clear that, once in power, it needed to take on board the demands WEL had made during the campaign.

From its beginning, sections of the women's movement began to make clear demands on the new Labor Government. As a consequence of the conjunction of an active women's movement and a reforming Labor Government, there was a period of rapid change in relation to the feminist agenda in the years 1973 to 1975. Some of these changes, such as Commonwealth provision of child care, had been in train before the Labor Government was elected, but it consolidated and extended them. Others were genuine Labor Government initiatives. In April 1973, for example, amid much publicity, Elizabeth Reid was appointed to assist the Prime Minister on women's issues, and with this appointment, the modern femocrat phenomenon was born.

Feminists who had assumed governments would always oppose their demands found themselves in a new situation. The Whitlam Government had a policy of providing funds for community initiative in setting up new services; feminists soom realized these could include women's services – refuges for battered women, health and rape crisis centres, and so on. This sudden opportunity to gain government funds for feminist projects posed some tricky problems. For those in WEL, or from an active Labor Party background, it was relatively easy to adapt to the new situation and seek government funding for feminist purposes. But for those from further to the left, suspicious of the Labor Party from the 1960s and averse to any kind of involvement with the 'capitalist state', the contradictions were sharper. One might be sacrificing long-term independence and critique for short-term gain; one might be 'co-opted', made too moderate and prepared to compromise, by absorption into the functions of the state. Worse still, there was the danger that, in the feminist refuges and health centres that sprang up all over the country, feminists were providing cheap or even free dedicated labour for services that ought to be fully government funded.

But these doubts soon affected only a minority of feminists. Most came to feel that real change in a feminist direction was indeed possible through the agency of the state. For a significant number of the educated professional women who loomed large in the feminist movement and engaged in these debates, the state emerged as a significant employer. As Marian Sawer points out, in the decade that followed Reid's appointment the number of femocrats rose markedly. In July 1974, when a Women's Affairs section was established in the

From left to right: Helen L'Orange; the Hon Justice Elizabeth Evatt; Her
Excellency Mrs Mervat Tallawy; the Prime Minister, the Hon P. J. Keating,
MP; the Hon Wendy Fatin, MP; Quentin Bryce; Kaye Loder; Anne Summers

Department of Prime Minister and Cabinet, feminists such as Lyndall Ryan and Sara Dowse were appointed. The process of creating women's, indeed feminist, policy positions continued under the new Coalition (Fraser) Government, which in 1976 made the Women's Affairs Branch the nucleus of a network of women's policy units in various departments (Sawer, 1990). Although the number of such units later declined, the principle of policy advice within departments linked to a central co-ordinating unit remained.

The fall of the Labor Government in November 1975 meant a slowing down from the frenetic pace of change and reform at Federal level that had characterized the previous three years. Nevertheless, most of the major gains of the Whitlam years were consolidated, and there were some important developments in several states. The pattern emerged that the women's movement made most headway under Labor governments, at either State or Federal level, and, while experiencing some setbacks when Liberal governments came in, were frequently able to maintain and at times extend gains even under less sympathetic governments.

This pattern is strikingly evident in, to take just one example, the case of equal employment opportunity. An historic change occurred right at the beginning of the Whitlam Government period, with the

Arbitration Commission's Equal Pay decision of December 1972. The new women's movement's attention turned increasingly towards attempting to achieve, through the agency of state, equal opportunity in employment, which meant full access to jobs formerly done only or largely by men, and access to the same chances as men of promotion to higher positions. The prime movers in this strategy were not so much the radicals who had been in Women's Liberation, but rather the liberal feminists, working in WEL and other similar organizations. Progress was made more easily at the State rather than the Federal level, especially, but not only, in states with Labor governments. The New South Wales Act in 1980 gave the Office of the Director of Equal Opportunity in Public Employment the power to require government authorities to develop equal opportunity management plans, and to take steps to increase the hiring and promotion of target groups, at that time women, migrants of non-English-speaking-background, and Aborigines, with people with physical disabilities being added in 1983.

A great deal of feminist energy was poured into attempting to make the new legislation work. Many became the Equal Opportunity Officers required by the Act; countless more served on equal opportunity committees within their place of work, acting as a pressure group for women's hiring and promotion within the organization. Feminism, with the powers of the state behind it, was able to make real headway in changing both attitudes and practices connected with employment within the public sector, and to a lesser degree within the private sector as well.

Feminists on feminism and the state

By the end of the 1980s, Australian feminists had had seventeen years of femocratic experience, and at least two decades of continuous feminist debate. During the 1980s there was discussion of feminist theory and the state, especially in edited collections, such as Cora Baldock and Bettina Cass's *Women, Social Welfare and the State*, Dorothy Broom's *Unfinished Business: Women and Social Justice* (1984), and Marian Simms's *Australian Women and the Political System* (1984). In addition, the journal *Refractory Girl* during the mid-1980s carried discussion papers written by a number of key academics-turned-femocrats. But it is in the last three years that there has truly been a flood of books and articles attempting to assess the effects of the Australian feminist engagement with the state, to draw theoretical conclusions about what had happened, and to test feminist theoretical debates against practical experience (Franzway *et al.*, 1989; S. Watson, 1990; Yeatman, 1990; Poiner and Wills, 1991; Sawer, 1990; Eisenstein, 1991).

The intersections between theory production and political experience are complex. On the one hand, there is indeed a connexion. The flood of Australian books of recent years discussing feminism and the state clearly has much to do with the intersection between feminist politics and feminist theory.[4] On the other hand, theoretical debates do have their own trajectory, as debate in a given area is influenced by a broad theoretical field, by American, British, or French theory, as much as by direct knowledge of particular Australian practice.

Feminist debates about the state have occurred in a context where feminist theory is increasingly being produced inside the academy. In the 1970s and 1980s, the disciplines came, one after the other, in history, philosophy, literature, sociology, anthropology, political science, under feminist scrutiny and challenge. The demands for university courses which studied feminist theory grew, and gradually courses sprang up everywhere, both special interdisciplinary women's studies courses, or courses focusing on women and feminist theory within the established disciplines. The result is that where, in the early 1970s, feminist theory was read, discussed and produced in activist feminist groups, by the 1980s and 1990s it is more likely to be produced in the academy itself. To emphasize the role of the academy in the production of feminist theory is not to suggest its isolation from feminist politics; indeed feminist academics have played a significant role in public debate and community action. Much of the burst of analysis of recent years has come from women who have had a dual experience, having worked both as academics and as femocrats: Clare Burton, Sue Wills, Gretchen Poiner, Carol O'Donnell, Hester Eisenstein, Lyndall Ryan, Marian Sawer. Practically all of it bears the fruit of a combination of feminist theorizing and debate with a sustained reflection on the specifically Australian political context.

The question that has exercised the most attention is that of how we can assess the success of feminist engagement with the state. Some important analyses, especially by those who have had experience as femocrats themselves, give a largely positive accounting of the femocrat phenomenon. In *Sisters in Suits*, Marian Sawer, for example, describes the level of government-funded services in Australia run by women for women as 'remarkable by global standards and far above that in Britain or the United States' (1990: 251). She includes as success stories government recognition of feminist analyses and programmes on issues such as domestic violence, child sexual abuse, women's health issues, community-based child care, training and education programmes for women who have been out of the workforce, the dramatic rise of women's participation in higher education, and the achievement of greater rights and participation (but not earnings, she says, rather questionably) in the workplace.

Even greater, in Sawer's estimation, is Australian feminist achievement in the realm of bureaucratic innovation. Feminist success in the bureaucracy is characterized as a quiet revolution: 'Over the last fifteen years Australian women have created a range of women's policy machinery . . . which is unrivalled elsewhere. . . . By 1988, Australian women had won a growing international reputation for the kind of policy mechanisms they had developed.' She praises Australian feminists for developing mechanisms which were consistent with feminist philosophy; a centre-periphery model, with the hub in the major co-ordinating government department and spokes in functional depart- ments, a network of policy units rather than a separate, vertically- integrated, women's policy department. 'The wheel of women's affairs, in which functional experts examine policy at its point of origin for its impact on women, backed up by a strong co-ordinating body with access to all Cabinet submissions, has been,' says Sawer, 'a characteristically Australian contribution' (1990: xv-xvi; see also Eisenstein, 1991).

Many other commentators have been more critical. A common thread in these more negative assessments is that feminist apparent successes have involved an increase in the powers of the state in individual lives, a decrease in family and collective power, and a giving of benefits to white, middle-class women rather than to women as a whole. There is a rejection of the notion of distinctive 'women's interests', which can be uniformly affected by particular governmental policies and practices (Pringle and Watson, 1992: 69). Gretchen Poiner and Sue Wills, in *The Gifthorse* (1991), offer a very sober assessment indeed of Equal Employment Opportunity legislation, seeing it as having benefited some, but having little effect for the majority. Anna Yeatman's *Bureaucrats, Technocrats, Femocrats* (1990) has an interest- ing and critical analysis of femocracy. She sees the problem which faces all femocrats, their fundamental dilemma, as being that the feminist strategies they propose will tend, whatever their intentions and class sympathies, to suit the interests of middle-class women like themselves. Ideas such as affirmative action and equal opportunity, for example, are helpful only for those already with education and recognized skill. Further, femocrat successes operate in firmly circumscribed aspects of state activity. Yeatman shows the gender divison within the middle and upper levels of the public service, women being more readily employed in 'soft' areas such as child care, health services, social security and social welfare, and education, while men continue to dominate the 'hard' areas such as economic and financial policy, foreign affairs, immi- gration, trade, defence, policing, labour and industrial relations.

Feminism, liberalism and postmodernism

These attempts to interpret the Australian femocrat experiment have led directly to the more theoretical question of the limits and possibili- ties of liberal feminism itself. Feminist theorists ask whether feminism is a form of liberal theory, or its most powerful modern critic. Some argue that it is both, Pauline Johnson, for example, describing feminism as placed in 'a complex double relation to liberal thought' (1991: 67). Suzanne Franzway, Di Court, and Bob Connell, in their book *Staking a Claim: Feminism, Bureaucracy, and the State* (1989), also point to the two-sidedness of liberal theory for feminism. From its beginnings feminism relied on the Enlightenment ideal of the citizen, supposedly universal, free and equal, refining it to include women as well as men. In modern Australia liberal feminism has provided the arguments about unequal treatment and unequal access which form the basis for anti-discrimination legislation and the provision of women's services. On the other hand, Franzway, Court and Connell point out, liberal theory has no *social* theory to explain the sexual inequalities and oppressions that do indeed arise.

Postmodernism presents feminism with some interesting problems. In postmodernist discourse, the Enlightenment is perceived as white mythology, an imperial project assuming Western male reason as mode and model for humanity. Against this illusory universalism, poststructuralism and postmodernism stress difference, of gender, culture, identity. Feminism faces a conflict between an Enlightenment ideal that appears to promise women freedom through equality and universality, and a postmodernist critique of that ideal, promising freedom through plurality and diversity.

Feminism has, however, always faced this conflict. Although poststructuralist commentators rarely acknowledge it, many aspects of their critique have a history in Romanticism and its critique of the Enlightenment. Since the end of the eighteenth century, Romanticism has presented, as Ursula Vogel puts it, 'an aesthetic ideal of the many-faceted human personality in whom all faculties – reason and feeling, spirituality and sensuality – are fully and harmoniously developed' (Vogel, 1986: 19). For two centuries Romanticism has placed variety above uniformity, the particular above the universal. The political sphere is regarded as marginal, infinitely less important than that of unconventional desires which point towards the utopia of a regenerated world. Romanticism represents a quest for individuality, diversity and organic wholeness. It enjoys the diversity of male and female as a source of energy. It revels in the contrasts, conflict, exchanges and inversionary possibilities of bodily difference and sensuous desire. Apart from the utopian notion of organic wholeness, so discredited now, how familiar all this sounds, in our current end-of-a century feeling of fragmentation and dissonance.

Carole Pateman has been the most powerful proponent of the argument that liberalism cannot be made compatible with feminism. A key figure in feminist political theory internationally, Pateman left Australia for the US in the late 1980s. Her major works, most notably in this context *The Sexual Contract* (1988), do not refer in detail to Australian feminist debates, and very little of her work has appeared in Australian feminist journals or has been published in Australia. Yet her work does bear the influence of Australian feminist experiences, with its consistent concern with the question of how feminists might argue for the possibility of change through the agency of government. And her ideas have certainly been influential within Australian feminist discussion of liberal theory and the state.

Pateman argues that liberalism, being grounded in a fraternal, exclusively male, social contract, cannot provide a basis for women to take an equal place in a patriarchal civil order. In refusing bodily and other difference, liberalism cannot generate the conditions for women's freedom. As a result, while feminism has often been seen as a continuation of liberalism, an extension of liberal principles and rights to women as well as men, it inevitably challenges liberalism itself. In Pateman's argument, the social contract of liberal theory was made not by individuals, as usually supposed, but by brothers, a fraternity, by men who share a bond *as men*. In short the contract guarantees the rule of men over women: through it the brothers appropriate women's ability to give birth. Women, Pateman maintains, are still excluded from the central category of 'the individual', the bedrock of contractarian doctrine. Her solutions are for women and men to address sexual difference politically, rather than repress it in the name of a hypothetical non-sexed individual. The achievement of legal equality and freedom becomes then not the end of feminism but rather the precondition for the development of women's autonomy, where women become free as women, rather than as like men.

Pateman's argument has some difficulties. She comes dangerously close to reducing liberalism to its presumed origin, as if its end, its goal, its possibilities are necessarily exhausted and limited by its conceptual and historical beginnings. The form of liberalism she is addressing is closer to that of the American individualist tradition than to the corporate 'new liberalism' which underlies both the Australian welfare state and modern Australian liberal feminism.[5] In addition, her argument rests on a unitary conception of women, an 'autonomous femininity', a set of definable female interests and demands that will be different from men's. A key question confronting feminists seeking political change – will the reforms they seek benefit women generally, or some at the expense of others? – cannot be addressed in this binary framework. While questions of class and race are from time to time noted in Pateman's work, they are not seen as having relevance in the sphere of sexual difference and sexual relations. That sphere is characterized by sex and gender alone.

From 'the state' to 'citizenship'

Related to the debate over feminism's success or failure, and what this means for liberal feminist ideals, is the question of how feminist theory should understand the state generally. What do, or can, we mean by 'the state'? Can there be a distinctively feminist conception of the state? Does feminist theory need a concept of the state at all?

Speaking from an unambiguously radical feminist position, Judith Allen answers the last question in the negative: feminism does not need the concept, the category, at all. She rejects those feminist theories of the state which see it as guaranteeing male power, on the basis that male power is everywhere, and does not need the state. Feminists who attempt to argue that the state can be used for feminist ends are equally opposed, on the grounds that they use 'the state' to cover sites for struggle too diverse to be characterized together. Those practices we often talk about as part of the state – government, policing, bureaucracy – are better thought of as within broader zones of phallocentric culture (Allen, 1990).

Most other commentators, however, continue to discuss 'the state' and make various suggestions as to how feminism should theorize it. Franzway, Court and Connell see the state as constituted by gender (as well as class) relations, an *agent* in sexual politics acting quintessentially in a public realm culturally marked as masculine. Sophie Watson and Rosemary Pringle, by contrast, describe the state not as an agent but as a set of *arenas*, a collection of *practices*, operating on the basis of already existing power relations, a by-product of political struggles. Jan Pettman, working towards a feminist theory of international relations, characterizes states as 'historical, contingent, and ongoing projects', and state-making as a process of establishing and maintaining centralized authority over territory and population (Pettman, 1992b).

Many feminists have tended to see the state as an arena of political practice which feminist political activists could choose or refuse to enter. The choice is often construed as one of ineffective purity outside, versus contaminated effectiveness inside. Sophie Watson typically asked in the introduction to her book, *Playing the State* (1990): Have feminist demands been diluted or co-opted through engagement with the institutions and discourses which constitute the state? In view of the poststructuralist argument, put most strongly by Derrida, that we cannot stand outside the concepts we critique, perhaps we need now to deconstruct the terms of this question. We can no longer conceive of the state as something outside us, and retain that impossible (modernist, oppositional) dream of a pure feminism, born outside the state, contemplating entering into it to achieve its own ends.

Perhaps in recognition of these dilemmas, or perhaps in response to a changed political context, there has in any case been a recent reorientation within feminist debates from theorizing the state to theorizing citizenship. There has been a shift of interest from the problem of how to characterize the state to one of *deconstructing the idea of the citizen who inhabits that state*, from a focus on social structure (the state) to one on political discourse and culture (citizenship). The main shift in emphasis has been to look not so much at the structural limitations to women's freedom and liberation, as at competing attempts, feminist and anti-feminist, to define and expand or limit women's sphere of political activity, at women's political agency.

Yet the focus on citizenship, on legal, political and social rights, leads us back, once again, via a different route, to a concern with the powers, constitution and boundaries of the state. Who belongs, and what do we belong to? As readers of *Feminist Review* will know better than I can, this question is being asked with a new urgency in Europe, where boundaries and state entities are shifting, and where ethnic and national loyalties are changing the political structure of Europe with great rapidity. The same question is also being asked, very sharply, and in a different way, in the former 'colonies of settlement', in Canada, New Zealand, the United States and Australia. In these societies, in distinctive ways and to different degrees, indigenous peoples are demanding sovereignty, compensation, and self-determination, seeking not only general citizenship rights, but also particular indigenous rights, as prior owners and occupants of the countries in which they live.

In Australia, the debate is rapidly shifting. In a landmark judgement of the Supreme Court in June 1992, known as the Mabo decision, certain forms of native land title have been recognized in Australian law for the first time. The constitutional implications are enormous and still only dimly recognized. Aboriginal demands for land rights and sovereignty, some form of independent government within the larger polity, are slowly forcing a recognition by the rest of the population, immigrants and their descendants, British and non-British, male and female, conservative and socialist, nationalist and internationalist, feminist and non-feminist, that we are all invaders and occupiers still.[6] This recognition is all the more confronting and difficult in a context where Aboriginal and non-Aboriginal people do not form clear binary opposites, but are interconnected inextricably, through descent, history and culture, through sexual, personal, economic, and political relationships, in virtually every way. Rhetorics of national identity, as the example of Paul Keating so clearly and interestingly indicates, in this context veer between a search for appropriate forms of acknowledging and respecting distinct and different rights and claims, and a desire for a multiple, plural inclusiveness, where neither distinctness nor hybrid inclusiveness quite satisfies 'our' contradictory desires and history.

Such Aboriginal demands present to non-Aboriginal Australian feminists a challenge to our conceptual view of the world far more profound than previously understood. There have, of course, always been different political positions on Aboriginal-feminist issues. Non-Aboriginal feminists have disagreed sharply over how to respond to gender-based conflict within Aboriginal communities, on issues such as domestic violence and rape in particular. On the whole, their view is to wait for Aboriginal women's requests for support or comment. The most common approach amongst non-Aboriginal feminists has been one of attempting to respect (not always successfully) the specificity of Aboriginal women's demands and needs separately but *within* an overall conception of redressing the wrongs of women generally. Feminist agencies within government, such as the Federal Office for the Status of Women, have, for example, to some degree consulted with Aboriginal women to develop specific policies on questions concerning employment opportunities, child care, violence against women, and so forth. Equal opportunity legislation, developed primarily to meet the demands of 'women' in general, includes 'Aboriginal people' (along with other specified groups) as a distinct target group, but is generally of little value to them, so profound are their disadvantages in the labour market (Poiner and Wills, 1991: 94–6).

Roberta Sykes from Queensland addresses a meeting of Aborigines outside Parliament House

After recent events, however, such as the Mabo decision on land rights, and the growing though uneven acceptance by non-Aboriginal Australians of their responsibilities for the past (dispossession itself, brutality, murder, exploitation, institutionalization, family break-up), feminists are starting to realize that Aboriginal demands cannot be contained within the existing feminist framework , and that the entire political framework within which femocrats operate is under question, and liable to change. 'The state', for Australian feminism, has itself become potentially unstable, as the implications of respecting Aboriginal sovereignty in a context where Aboriginal people form a small (less than 2 per cent) and widely dispersed section of the population begin to be thought through. And so the older question, 'can we achieve feminist goals directly through the agencies of the state?', gives way to a new (for us) question: 'what kind of state should we be attempting to construct?'

In the debate over Aboriginal sovereignty and the constitution of the state, land title, political rights and national identity, feminists will of course be trying to find ways to develop and maintain a feminist perspective. One of the most important contributions is Jan Pettman's recent book, *Living in the Margins: Racism, Sexism and Feminism in*

Australia (1992a), which summarizes in a clear and comprehensive fashion debates over national identity, the colonial encounter, migration, Aboriginal history and politics, the role of academics and feminist debates. Yet so fast is the pace of change, after the Mabo decision and the positive response of the Federal Labor Government to the challenge posed by the UN Year of Indigenous Peoples, that already the issues have shifted. Pettman argues that feminists must move beyond category politics, and develop an inclusive political project, that is feminist, anti-racist and anti-colonialist. What is interesting now is that it just may be that feminism, if it is to survive as a major political, social and cultural force in Australia, may have no alternative.

Notes

Ann Curthoys is Professor of Social History at the University of Technology, Sydney, New South Wales, Australia. She has been active in the Australian women's movement since 1970, and has published in a wide range of fields including feminist theory, women's history, media history and the history of Aboriginal-European relations, anti-immigration movements, and the anti-war movement of the 1960s. Her book, *For and Against Feminism: A Personal Journey into Feminist Theory and History*, was published by Allen & Unwin in 1988.

1 Letter published in *Sydney Morning Herald*. In the published version, the letter had been edited to delete the word 'countries' from the original, the Aboriginal activist use of the word 'countries', denoting Aboriginal 'nations', not being understood by the Letters editor.
2 SMH, 28.2.92.
3 I met Keating earlier this year; one could not but notice the depth of his fervent nationalism and his hatred of the 'conservative establishment'. Meaghan Morris discusses Keating thus: 'In the late 1980s, I came to be aware of feeling an entirely new emotion: adulation of a national leader. I felt it in the comic-ironic mode that is culturally natural to Australians of my general social background (mixed working-class and petit-bourgeois Irish-Australian). . . . Of course, my "entirely new" emotion may well involve something that I have read about precisely in relation to other people – in the past, and in countries where it is respectable, even normal (as it is not in Australia) to wave flags, cheer parades, and praise the nation' (1992: 22–5).
4 Mary Maynard commented after her study tour of Australia in 1991 that Australian feminism was much more engaged than is British feminism with theorizing the state, a result, she thought, of our much closer participation in it. Paper to the Sir Robert Menzies Australian Studies Centre, University of London, London, October 1991.
5 I am indebted for this point to Marian Sawer, who made it during the discussion following my presentation of an earlier version of this paper at the 'Women and the State' symposium at the Australian Historical Association Conference, Canberra, 30 September 1992.
6 I have also discussed this issue in 'Identity crisis: colonialism, nation, and gender in Australian history' *Gender and History* 5: 2, (1993).

References

ALLEN, Judith (1990) 'Does feminism need a theory of the state?' in Sophie Watson (1990).

CURTHOYS, Ann (1993) 'Identity crisis: colonialism, nation, and gender in Australian history' *Gender and History*. Vol. 5 No 2.

EISENSTEIN, Hester (1991) *Gender Shock* Sydney: Allen & Unwin.

FRANZWAY, S., COURT, D., and CONNELL, R. W. (1989) *Staking a Claim: Feminism, Bureaucracy, and the State* Sydney: Allen & Unwin.

JOHNSON, Pauline (1991) 'Feminism and liberalism' *Australian Feminist Studies* 14 (Summer) 1991.

LAKE, Marilyn (1986) 'The politics of respectability: identifying the masculinist context', *Historical Studies* 86 (May) 1986.

MORRIS, Meaghan (1992) 'Ecstasy and economics', *Discourse* 14/2 (Spring/ Summer) 1992.

PETTMAN, Jan (1992a) *Living in the Margins: Racism, Sexism and Feminism in Australia* Sydney: Allen & Unwin.

—— (1992b) 'Women, nationalism and the state: towards an international feminist perspective' *Gender and Development Studies* Bangkok: Asian Institute of Technology.

POINER, Gretchen and WILLS, Sue (1991) *The Gifthorse: A Critical look at Equal Employment Opportunities in Australia* Sydney: Allen & Unwin.

PRINGLE, Rosemary and WATSON, Sophie (1992) '"Women's interests" and the post-structuralist state' in Michele Barrett and Anne Phillips (1992) editors, *Destabilizing Theory: Contemporary Feminist Debates* Cambridge: Polity Press: 53–73.

REEKIE, Gail (1992) 'Contesting Australia' in Gillian Whitlock and David Carter (1992) editors, *Images of Australia* St Lucia: University of Queensland Press.

SAWER, Marian (1990) *Sisters in Suits: Women and Public Policy in Australia* Sydney: Allen & Unwin.

SPEARRITT, Peter (1988) 'Celebration of a nation: the triumph of spectacle' in Susan Janson and Stuart Macintyre (1988) editors, *Making the Bicentenary*, a special issue of *Australian Historical Studies* Vol. 23, No. 91.

SUMMERS, Anne (1975) *Damned Whores and God's Police: The Colonisation of Women in Australia* Ringwood: Penguin.

SYDNEY MORNING HERALD (SMH) (1992) January–December.

VOGEL, Ursula (1986) 'Rationalism and romanticism: two strategies for women's liberation' in Evans *et al.* (1986) editors, *Feminism and Political Theory* London: Sage Publications.

WATSON, Don (1979) *Brian Fitzpatrick: A Radical Life* Sydney: Hale & Iremonger.

WATSON, Sophie (1990) editor, *Playing the State: Australian Feminist Interventions* London: Verso.

YEATMAN, Anna (1990) *Bureaucrats, Technocrats, Femocrats: Essays on the Contemporary Australian State* Sydney: Allen & Unwin.

REMAPPING AND RENAMING:
New Cartographies of Identity, Gender and Landscape in Ireland

Catherine Nash

Introduction

In discussing Mahasweta Devi's story 'Douloti the Bountiful', Gayatri Chakravorty Spivak describes the story's ending. Douloti, the daughter of an Indian tribal bonded worker, is sold into bonded prostitution in order to repay her father's loan. Devastated by venereal disease, she dies walking to hospital, having lain down on the comfort of the bare earth where the local schoolmaster had drawn the map of India in order to teach his students nationalism in preparation for Independence Day. The next morning the schoolmaster and his students find Douloti on the map (Spivak, 1992a). This tension between the assertion of national identity in the postcolonial nation and the presence of the female subaltern, can be paraphrased as a problematic relationship between the map and the body. The map in Devi's story stands as a symbol of the national territory, the geographic outline both constituting and symbolizing the 'imagined community' of the nation (Anderson, 1983).

In considering contemporary Irish culture, I am concerned not only to consider the issue of identity in relation to both feminism and postcolonialism, but to raise the issue of 'place' and its intersection with identity. The issue of place operates at the abstract level of the nation. It also concerns the visual relationship to place associated with the concept of 'landscape' (Rose, 1992), and the sensual, lived experience of the local environment. In contemporary critical writing, spatial metaphors – the terms position, place, site, space, ground, field, territory, terrain, margin, periphery and map – recur (Diprose and Ferrell, 1991; Tagg, 1992). The metaphor of mapping functions at a number of levels. It stands most commonly for a positioning on a theoretical and ideological plane. It also describes a location within geographical space. In the relationship between the Western and Third Worlds, this is not unconnected to theoretical position. It can be taken to conceptualize diverse ways of representing space, in textual, visual and multidimensional artistic, and conventional cartographic media. In my discussion in this article of the relationship between identity, gender, the body and the map through the work of the Irish artist Kathy Prendergast, I retain the reference to geographic space by my use of a mapping metaphor. This metaphor is mobilized, not to distinguish between the 'real' and 'imagined' space of the nation, but to make clear that it refers to more than purely theoretical positioning.

A final introductory point to make is that since notions of race, gender and identity are being treated as culturally and historically formulated constructs throughout this article, they are presented without inverted commas. (Butler, 1990; Epstein and Straub, 1992; Smith, 1992; Weedon, 1987) Through a discussion of issues arising in the work of Kathy Prendergast, this article raises the possibility of a feminist and postcolonial identification with place which avoids the biologism and essentialism of the idea of a natural, organic and intuitive closeness to nature in the former and a native, childlike and racial closeness to nature in the latter.

I chose the terms remapping and renaming for the title of this article, firstly to draw attention to issues of landscape and language, and the ways in which they are tied to issues of gender in the negotiation of ideas of Irish identity, and secondly, to highlight the way in which forms of cultural expression which deal with national identity in this postcolonial context, do so in relation to the early construction of Irishness in response to the colonial experience. The colonial mapping of Ireland in the nineteenth century, the concurrent Anglicization of Irish place names, and the decline of the Irish language provide the historical background for the expression of themes of cultural loss and recovery in contemporary Irish culture. Both the act of naming and mapping assert the power of representation. Attempts to rename and remap claim this power to recover an authentic identity and relationship to place. The contemporary use of the map and place name prompts a consideration of the commonly accepted links between gender, language, landscape and identity, yet the shift from colony to independence did not entail the redundancy of discourses of male power; rather, these were transposed and translated into new forms within Irish nationalist discourse (Smyth, 1991).

Geography and gender

Issues of geography and gender arise in the work of Kathy Prendergast, one of the younger generation of Irish artists who have adopted a critical, ironic and sometimes humorous approach to traditional Irish landscape art. In using the map motif, her work raises connexions between landscape and the female body, between the political control of landscape and territory and the control of female sexuality. Prendergast rejects the interpretation of her images as feminist statements and describes the work as a representation of a 'personal geography' (Hanrahan, 1991: 6). The work can, however, be discussed as an instance where the tension between this 'personal geography' of the body and the space of the national landscape is manifest. In a series of drawings of 1983, as in other work by Kathy Prendergast, accepted scales are confused, references to other artistic conventions are employed. She uses a device of creative interplay between words and image, of detailed cross-sections and plans of a female body (Douglas Hyde Gallery, 1990). In 'Enclosed Worlds in Open Spaces' (Figure 1) the drawing of a truncated female body evokes cartographic conventions of grid lines, compass point and ships on the sea surrounding the body/land. The style of geomorphological, surveying or civil-engineering diagrams and plans is used in 'To Control a Landscape – Irrigation' (Figure 2), 'To Control a Landscape – Oasis' (Figure 3) and 'To Alter a Landscape' (Figure 4). These conventions are conflated with the styles of anatomical and gynaecological diagrams. In the drawings, operations of control, manipulation and alteration are in process on and within the passive land/body. In their dissection of the female body they evoke anatomical drawings of female organs which functioned in the medico-moral politics of the late nineteenth century. The quietness of the images in their carefully drawn style, their reference to yellowed historical maps and navigational charts, make the violence of the subject matter more powerful. In using several registers of representation such as the cartographic, geological and medical, the drawings are complex multilayered texts which do not provide a sealed and completed set of meanings to be consumed but engage the viewer in the making of meanings. The images draw us in as explorers, navigators, engineers, in search of fullness, wholeness and simplicity of meaning, only to disrupt the process of reasoning and understanding in their ambiguity, 'the un-naming power of ambiguity' (Prentice, 1986: 70). The familiarity of the connexion between colonial control of other lands and the control of female sexuality and the use of gender in the discourse of discovery and territorial expansion, is displaced by the powerful subtlety of these images (Kolodny, 1975; Montrose, 1991).

Kathy Prendergast draws on traditions of representation of women in order to deconstruct their supposed neutrality. It is her ironic position as a female artist in relation to these traditions that gives Prendergast's reinscriptions their counterstrategic power. The artist's use of the idea of land and landscape and its relationship to control of the feminine is understandable in the historical context of colonial efforts to control 'an essentially feminine race' and post–independence attempts to employ notions of femininity, rural life and landscape in the construction of Irishness and the subordination of Irish women (Cairns and Richards, 1988). Issues of gender and national identity intersect in multiple ways; in the gendering of the concept of the nation, in the idea of the national landscape as feminine, in the concern with issues of race, place, and the national population and the delimiting of gender roles in the

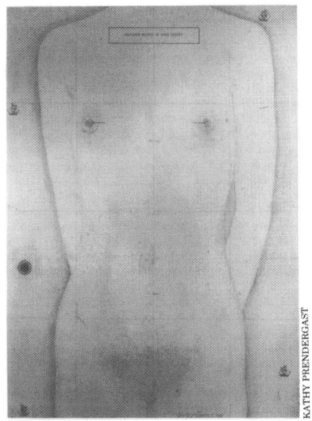

Kathy Prendergast. Enclosed Worlds in Open Spaces

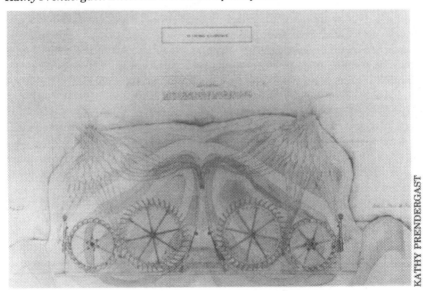

Kathy Prendergast. To Control a Landscape – Irrigation

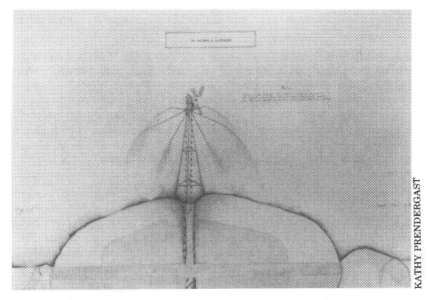

Kathy Prendergast. To Control a Landscape – Oasis

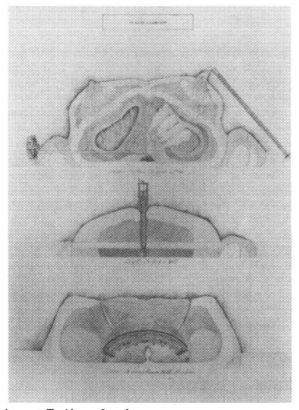

Kathy Prendergast. To Alter a Landscape

idealization and representation of rural life. The symbolism of Ireland as female derives from the sovereignty goddess figure of early Irish tradition, the personification of this goddess in the figures of Irish medieval literature and the allegorization of Ireland as woman in the eighteenth-century classical poetic genre, the *aisling*, following colonial censorship of the expression of direct political dissent (O'Brien Johnson and Cairns, 1991b: 3). It also relates to the colonial feminization of Ireland and the Irish which was adopted, adapted and contested within nationalist discourse (Butler Cullingford, 1990; Cairns and Richards 1987, 1988). The continued use of the notion of Ireland as female, against which male poets assert both personal and national identity (Riordan, 1985) endorses and strengthens the signifying use of women in Ireland, their erosion from Irish history and contemporary silencing (Boland, 1989). Traditional landscape representations in Ireland are imbued with conceptions of both national and gender identity, most significantly in the imagery of the West of Ireland (Nash, 1993).

'Women of the West': gender, nation and landscape in early twentieth-century Ireland

In the construction of the image of the West of Ireland in the first decades of the twentieth century, many of these intersections of gender, landscape and nation are manifest. The image of the West stands at the centre of a web of discourses of racial and cultural identity, femininity, sexuality and landscape which were being used in attempts to secure cultural identity and political freedom. The construction of the West must be seen both in the context of Irish history and culture, and within the broader context of the anti-modernism and romantic primitivism of the period, of European discourses concerning racial degeneration, eugenics, evolution and environmentalism, spiritualism and rural regeneration, and the particular context of Irish nationalist attempts to revitalize and revivify the nation. These discourses intersected with the idea of national identity and gravitated around notions of place and landscape. Images of the peasant women of the West in travel writing and photography, literature and painting, were one set of several versions of femininity being contested at the time, as part of a set of discourses which participated in the negotiation and inscription of ideas of femininity and, through femininity, the future ideal form of Irish society. The Irish suffrage movement was at this time posing questions about the role of women in political life and within the independent state, as were the women's military nationalist organizations (Ward, 1983; Owens, 1984; Murphy, 1989). This threat to the male monopoly of political power by politically active women intensified the drive to fix the role, position and the very nature of womanhood. These issues over-lapped with concerns of cultural purity and preservation, centred on the image of the West of Ireland as an Irish cultural region, whose physical landscape provided the greatest contrast to the landscape of

Englishness (Nash, 1993). On to the body of the peasant woman were focused concerns over racial, sexual and cultural purity and the social and moral organization of a future independent Ireland.

The visual iconography of the West as an archetypal Irish land-scape was largely based on the paintings of Paul Henry, whose work was part of a tradition of European early modernist cultural primitivism which sought spirituality, stability and authenticity in a move to the Celtic fringes. Henry's work was also indebted to the Anglo-Irish search for a sense of community and natural spirituality in the West. In line with both traditions, the women in Henry's painting became part of the visual iconography of the West and acted as emblems of an idea of femininity based on a supposedly natural identification with nature and the landscape (see Figure 5).

While primitivism afforded a limited, positive evaluation of the Irish West as a source of cohesion, simplicity, instinctiveness and an organic relationship between lifestyle and environment, the primitive was ultimately considered lower in a hierarchy of civilization. As constructions of the imperial centre, both art history and anthropology contributed to the production of primitivism as a discriminatory discourse which posits the 'other' as both an object for the artist's gaze and for analytic scrutiny (Hiller, 1991). The discourses which primi-tivized women and the colony were fused in the representation of the female colonial subject. Yet, as a result of nationalist anti-urbanism and anti-imperialism, this primitivizing continued in nationalist accounts of the West. The idea of the primitive was appropriated but positively evaluated against the urban, industrial, colonial power. This primitiviz-ation of the West and of women, which had as a strong element the supposed unsuppressed instinctiveness, sexuality and unselfconscious sensuality of the primitive, had to be reconciled with the use of women by cultural nationalists as signifiers of moral purity and sexual innocence.

While convergences can be noted between the colonial appropri-ation of the landscape of the colony and the production of the subject woman, the codes of representation of both the peasant woman and the West as landscapes of desire were re-employed in nationalist writing. In the shift from emphasis on Celtic to Gaelic, the feminine was rejected as epitomizing the national character. Instead, ideas of anti-urbanism, nationalism, concern about the body, health and physique, were projected on to the woman's body, and against England as urban, industrial and debased. The emphasis on dress in the description of the people of the West corresponds to the importance of dress as a marker of national identity, constructed from elements of race, class and geogra-phy (Parker *et al.*, 1992: 10). Its importance was testified to in the concern over national costume in the Gaelic revival movement, which amounted to a 'national dress debate' in the 1910s. In that movement, an emphasis on the red skirts of women was tied to the symbolism of the colour as an indication of vitality, to the belief in the national love of colour evident from ancient costume, and to the rejection of modern

Paul Henry. The Potato Diggers 1912

fashion, which was considered to restrict the female biological functions. The concern over dress can be understood in the context of the cultural and biological role which was afforded to women within Irish Nationalism. The celebration of the women of the West intersects with issues of concern with degeneration, anti-urbanism and the moral economy of the body, and the sexual politics of representation.

In later painting and travel photography, by contrast, the image of the young woman was usually absent, reflecting both the demographic structure of Irish rural society in the context of large-scale rural depopulation and also the problematic nature of representation of young women. In the context of the construction of femininity by cultural nationalists and later, Church and State, which denied women an autonomous sexuality in their idealization of asexual motherhood, the visual representation of the idealized country woman rested uneasily with the history of eroticized images of women in Western art. The young woman was replaced by the depiction of the old peasant women who could represent the successful outcome of a life lived in accordance with the demands of motherhood, as well as being emblematic of the traditions, folklore, language and way of life extolled in the state. Alternatively, the depiction of the peasant woman was replaced by the portrayal of Western men, who epitomized the Gaelic masculine ideal. Thus nationalist writers of the Irish Ireland movement, in reaction to the nineteenth-century construction of the Celtic as feminine, asserted masculinity as the essential characteristic of the 'Gael'. While the idea of 'woman' remained the embodiment of the national spirit and the allegorical figure for the land of Ireland, this land now became the domain of the overtly masculine. The West was redefined as Gaelic, masculine, wholesome, pragmatic and Catholic in contrast to the femininity and natural spirituality of the Celtic. This denial of the female was also linked to the control of sexuality by Catholicism. This moral code supported the economic and social system of family farming, which demanded the regulation of sexuality for the control of inheritance (Cairns and Richards, 1988). With the perceived threat of an autonomous female sexuality to this social order, the counterpart of the Gaelic male had to be the desexualized mother figure.

The cottage in the landscape came to carry the cultural weight of the idealization of traditional rural, family life and its fixed morality and gender roles. It became a surrogate for the depiction of the rural Irish woman and the values of motherhood, tradition and stability (see Figure 6). The cottage as 'cradle of the race' evoked the idea of women as preservers of the race, active only as nurturers and reproducers of the masculine Gael. The homosocial bonding of Irish nationalism depended upon the exclusion of women from the body politic, while its conception of the landscape as female facilitated a masculinist relationship to place. The discourses which confined women within the domestic sphere simultaneously conferred on them the responsibility of maintaining the national population. Women's function was to reproduce the bodies of the 'body politic', represented as masculine (Gatens, 1991). The

Paul Henry. Connemara Cottages

conflation of body and nation in Irish national discourse (which found more explicit expression in the contemporaneous British eugenics movement) provided a vehicle for the systematic expression of concern over this 'body politics' – the nation and the national population. Concerns over the national population were closely linked to ideas of landscape. The idea of an organic link between environment and people was utilized in discourses which employed scientific conceptions of current climatology and anthrogeography to discourage emigration (Livingstone, 1991, 1992; Stepan, 1985). Fears of loss of population were made more urgent by the associated loss of Irish-language speakers, cultural bearers and vigorous genetic stock from the West of Ireland. Concern over emigration fused issues of gender and race, as it was felt that loss of those who 'would have made the best mothers and wives' leaves 'at home the timid, the stupid, and the dull to help in the deterioration of the race and to breed sons as sluggish as themselves' (Russell, 1912: 67–8). Both ideas of racial pride and racial fears were thus projected on to the body of the woman.

The cottage as an 'Irish citadel' stood for a preservation and reproduction of Irish language, tradition and folklore, for which women were considered to have paramount responsibility in their capacity as childcarers. This of course echoes the role accorded to women within other nationalist movements (Yuval-Davis and Anthias, 1989). The cottage was also considered as the basic unit of a distinctive Irish settlement pattern and therefore symbolic of Irish social organization in opposition to English culture. Thus the isolated rural cottage represented the realization, both in the physical fabric of the landscape and in the moral and spiritual domain, of the ideal form of Irish society. Its depiction in Irish landscape painting participated in the construction of Irish identity and the gender identities upon which it relied. Representation of landscape in early twentieth-century Ireland was coded with meaning in terms of both national and gender identity.

Postcolonialism, feminism and landscape

Contemporary landscape imagery is forced to confront both its historical use in the colonial and early nationalist contexts, and the issues of race and gender implicit in such use. Both the colonial mapping of subject lands and the representation of women in patriarchy are forms of representation which seek to reinforce the stability of the controlling viewpoint and negate or suppress alternative views. The map can be read as a manifestation of a desire for control which operates effectively in the implementation of colonial policy. The strategies used in the production of the map – the reinscription, enclosure and hierarchization of space – provide an analogue for the acquisition, management and reinforcement of colonial power. In the cataloguing process the world is normalized, disciplined, appropriated and controlled (Huggen, 1989; Harley, 1988, 1992). The mapping of the Irish landscape did not merely function to ease administration but fixed the 'other' and neutralized the threat of difference by the apparent stability of the map's coherence (Andrews, 1975; Hammer, 1989a, 1989b). In the same way, the representation of women fixes their bodies as landscapes of control and signifying use. The map, which relies on a controlling viewpoint whose stability cannot be guaranteed, is revealed as covering over alternative spatial configurations, which indicate both the plurality of possible perspectives on, and the inadequacy of any single model of the world (Huggen, 1989).

Feminism and postcolonialism share a problematic relationship to postmodernism, with its appropriation of the critical insights of both and the erasure of their source and political efficacy (Tiffin, 1987b; Adam and Tiffin, 1991; Bondi and Domosh, 1992). Both postcolonialism and feminism are engaged in the conflict between a politics of identity and a politics of difference (Best and Kellner, 1991). The poststructuralist rejection of the humanist conception of a universal subject and a stable core of identity undermines the liberatory and consolidatory aims of both. Yet, however fraught with difficulty, the conception of identity within poststructuralist theory offers a way to consider feminist and postcolonial relationships to place which avoids the essentializing of masculinist and colonialist discourse. The issue of land and land ownership is central to the colonial situation, but is also important symbolically in the postcolonial context when identification with landscape and place is one of the prime sources of cultural identity. The association between national identity and landscape is thus manifest in the postcolonial literal and symbolic reappropriation of place. In postcolonial literature, the development or recovery of an effective relationship to place, after dislocation or cultural denigration by the supposedly superior cultural and racial colonial power, becomes a means to overcome the sense of displacement and crisis of identity (Gray, 1986; Ashcroft *et al.*, 1989).

Yet, as Annamaria Carusi writes, 'a discourse which includes in an un-ironic and un-parodic way terms such as "identity", "consciousness" and "origin" appears both regressive and reactionary from a poststructuralist point of view' (Carusi, 1991: 100) Thus the dual agenda of postcolonial texts becomes 'to continue the resistance to (Neo) colonialism through a deconstructive reading of its rhetoric and to retrieve and reinscribe those postcolonial social traditions that in literature issue forth on a thematic level, and within a realist problematic, as principles of cultural identity and survival' (Selmon, 1991: 5). Poststructuralism, in other words, does not disallow the *critical* use of the concept of identity. To problematize identity allows for a cultural use of ideas of landscape which can reject its use within colonialist discourse to stereotype the native as biologically linked to the natural landscape. Similarly, a feminist use of ideas of landscape and place must confront the dangers of essentialism within ecofeminism (Plumwood, 1988; Warren, 1987; King, 1990; Merchant, 1990) and accounts which view women's relationship to landscape in terms of innate biological and psychological structures (Norwood and Monk, 1987b; Rudnick, 1987), and deal with masculinist use of ideas of landscape (Rose, 1992). The recognition of the constructed nature of identity allows landscape to be used as a source of identification without implying a fixed, natural and inherent identity.

Renaming, gender and the postcolonial landscape

However important the use of landscape is in the postcolonial context, its use is problematic if it fails to address the issue of gender. In postcolonial Ireland, there has been much empirical research into place names. Their reinscription on the country's maps and their use as cultural metaphors combine two elements which are central to national identity: language and place. The attempt to recover the meaning and original form of a place name is often linked to a search for a recovery of a lost relationship to place, in Ireland expressed in a language no longer in majority use. The place name in Ireland carries cultural connotations which are being employed in a postcolonial exploration of identity, in which the place name carries the burden of a history of colonial loss of the Irish language, a history of population loss and emigration, and of colonial Anglicization of names of places in the nineteenth-century mapping project.

This contemporary use of the place name and the map prompts a consideration of the commonly accepted links between language, landscape and identity; of the question of attitudes to place; and of the possibility of recovery of meaning, of history and of authenticity.

In much contemporary Irish poetry ideas of landscape are employed. Places are named. This naming is linked to ideas of language loss. This decline of language is linked in turn to the loss of a distinctive lifestyle and a relationship to place considered to be more intimate and authentic than the present. For the writer, the evocative power of the place name provides a key to the shared social memory of a landscape whose collective meanings were part of a unifying repository of community knowledge, but which have been lost through loss of the language. Detailed place name research in Ireland is coloured by this sense of loss and recovery. The association of language and relationship to place depends upon the notion of a language as inherently appropriate for describing a particular landscape, and on the idea that words carry essential cultural essences. Yet the use of the Irish place name in poetry thus enables cultural difference to be inserted into the text (Ashcroft *et al.*, 1989).

However, this use becomes problematic when linked to gendered ideas of landscape, as in the work of Seamus Heaney, in which dualities of gender are fused to conceptions of politics, place and language. To a gendered consideration of the relationship between Ireland and England, Heaney adds a gendered view of language as symbolic also of difference. Poetic composition, for Heaney, is an 'encounter between masculine will and intelligence and feminine clusters of image and emotion', 'the feminine element' involving 'the matter of Ireland', and the masculine 'drawn from the involvement with English literature' (Heaney, 1980a: 34). This gender polarity is extended to a consideration of the way in which a place can be known. For Heaney, the two ways, one 'lived, illiterate and unconscious, the other learned, literate and conscious' correspond respectively to a Gaelic feminine, and to an Anglo-Saxon, masculine consciousness (Heaney, 1980a: 131). The place names which differentiate the cultural locales of the North represent the different ways of knowing the place through the language and syntax of the name. The Irish feminine language is soft, 'guttural' sensual and rich in vowel sounds. The planter's demesnes are 'staked out in consonants' (Heaney, 1980b: 27). Anahorish is a 'soft gradient/of consonant, vowel meadow' (Heaney, 1980b: 21). In the name Moyola 'the twaney guttural mater/spells itself . . . breathing its mists/through vowels and history' (Heaney, 1980b: 22).

While the idea of a female voice has important feminist uses, Heaney's use of the concept is problematic (Cameron, 1985). Heaney's poetry celebrates the feminine homeplace and mourns separation from it. It is against the construction of this landscape of the rural home as passive, organic and female that the poet, in distancing himself from it, can assert identity, activity and independence (Coughlan, 1991).

Deterritorializing identity

I have suggested above that the postcolonial and feminist commitment to concepts of identity and their securing through relationships to place risks reproducing the dualities of masculinist and colonial discourse. Though closeness to nature is positively evaluated, it leaves the culture/nature duality intact. This final section considers the possibility of a poststructuralist use of ideas of place which allows for multiple perspectives without undermining the strategic use of any one position. In 1991 Kathy Prendergast exhibited 'Land' (Figure 7, Curtis, 1991). It consisted of a canvas tent upon which the colours, lines and conventions of topographical mapping had been painted. The map as a flat, two-dimensional device was given volume and height. The map itself becomes the object of its representation. In this piece 'Land' has become the landscape itself which the map seeks to represent. This play between representation and its object undermines the idea of a simple equation between reality and representation. The authority of the map's representation is subverted. The relations between the 'natural' and the 'imitated' object are exposed as neither 'objective' representation nor even a 'subjective' reconstruction of the 'real' world, but as a play between alternative simulacra which problematize the easy distinction between object and subject (Huggen, 1989). The map in 'Land' becomes a shifting ground, a spatial metaphor which frees conceptions of identity and landscape from a repressive fixity and solidity.

KATHY PRENDERGAST

Kathy Prendergast, Land

In much writing on Ireland the landscape is tied down with its cultural threads, burdened with the weight of its historical and cultural load. In 'Land' the landscape and ideas of identity take flight, freed from the repressive fixity of identity. The land can symbolize the possibility of fluidity and openness, of multiple and diffuse 'names' and 'maps'. The map, as for Gilles Deleuze and Félix Guattari,

> is open and connectable in all its dimensions; it is detachable, reversible, susceptible to constant modification. It can be torn, reversed, adapted to any kind of mounting, re-worked by an individual, group or social formation. It can be drawn on the wall, conceived of as a work of art, constructed as a political action or as a meditation (Deleuze and Guattari, 1987: 12).

In this cartography the map is conceived as a rhizomatic ('open') rather than as a homogeneous ('closed') construct, which allows the emphasis to shift from de- to reconstruction, from map-breaking to map-making.

This use of the map allows for a culturally and historically located critique of colonial discourse and the possibility of alternative configurations of identity which are open, changeable and reworkable (Prentice, 1986). Similarly the body can be read as a text whose socially inscribed attributes function as part of a deployment of power. As Elizabeth Grosz writes, the body, as well as being the site of knowledge-power is 'also a site of resistance, for it exerts a recalcitrance, and always entails the possibility of counterstrategic reinscription, for it is capable of being self-marked, self-representated in alternative ways' (Grosz, 1990: 64). Both concepts of space and the body are open to multiple configuration. The recognition of the counterstrategic possibilities in the representation of the body and landscape which do not rely on fixed conceptions of identity allow the body/land relationship to be figured in multiple ways. The landscape can be transversed, journeyed across, entered into, intimately known, gazed upon. However tainted the concept of landscape is by colonial and masculinist discourse, a poststructuralist understanding of identity allows its reappropriation. Postcolonial and feminist remapping and renaming do not replace one authoritative representation with another but with multiple names and multiple maps.

Notes

An earlier version of this article was given as a paper at the conference 'Gender and Colonialism', University College, Galway, May 1992.

Catherine Nash is currently completing a Ph.D. on issues of landscape, gender and identity in Ireland in the twentieth century in the Departments of Geography and Art History at the University of Nottingham.

References

ADAM, Ian and TIFFIN, Helen (1991) editors, *Past the Last Post, Theorising Post Colonialism and Post Modernism* New York and London: Harvester Wheatsheaf.

ALCROFT, Linda (1988) 'Cultural feminism versus poststructuralism: the identity crisis in feminist theory' *Signs: Journal of Women in Culture and Society* Vol. 13, No. 3: 405–36.

ANDERSON, Benedict (1983) *Imagined Communities: Reflections on the Origin and Spread of Nationalism* London: Verso.

ANDREWS, John (1975) *A Paper Landscape* Oxford: Clarendon Press.

ASHCROFT, Bill *et al.* (1989) *The Empire Writes Back: theory and practice in post-colonial literatures* London: Routledge.

BEST, Steven and KELLNER, Douglas (1991) *Postmodern theory: critical interrogations* London: Macmillan.

BOLAND, Eavan (1989) *A kind of scar: the woman poet in a national tradition* Dublin: Attic Press.

BONDI, Liz and DOMOSH, Mona (1992) 'Other figures in other places: on feminism, postmodernism and geography' *Environment and Planning D, Society and Space* Vol. 10, No. 2: 199–213.

BUTLER CULLINGFORD, Elizabeth (1990) '"Thinking of her . . . as . . . Ireland": Yeats, Pearse and Heaney' *Textual Practice* 4, 1: 1–21.

BUTLER, Judith (1990) *Gender Trouble: Feminism and the Subversion of Identity* London: Routledge.

CAIRNS, David and RICHARDS, Shaun (1987) 'Woman in the discourse of celticism', *Canadian Journal of Irish Studies* 13, 1: 43–60.

—— (1988) *Writing Ireland: Colonialism, Nationalism and Culture* Manchester: Manchester University Press.

CAMERON, Deborah (1985) *Feminism and Linguistic Theory* London: Macmillan Press.

CARUSI, Annamaria (1991) 'Post, post and post, or, where is South African literature in all this?' in ADAM and TIFFIN (1991).

COUGHLAN, Patrica (1991) '"Bog Queens": the representation of women in the poetry of John Montague and Seamus Heaney' in O'BRIEN JOHNSON and CAIRNS (1991a).

CURTIS, Penelope (1991) editor, *Strongholds: New Art from Ireland* catalogue for the exhibition, 20 February-7 April 1991, Liverpool: Tate Gallery.

DELEUZE, Gilles and GUATTARI, Félix (1987) *A Thousand Plateaus: Capitalism and Schizophrenia* translated by Massumi, B., Minneapolis: University of Minnesota Press.

DIPROSE, Rosalyn and FERRELL, Robyn (1991) *Cartographies: poststructuralism and the mapping of bodies and spaces* Sydney: Allen & Unwin.

DOUGLAS HYDE GALLERY (1990) *Kathy Prendergast* (Exhibition catalogue with essay by Conor Joyce).

DRIVER, Felix and ROSE, Gillian (1992) *Nature and Science: Essays on the History of Geographical Knowledge* Historical Research Series, 28.

DURING, Simon (1985) 'Postmodernism or postcolonialism' *Landfall* Vol. 39, No. 3: 366–80.

EPSTEIN, Julia and STRAUB, Kristina (1992) editors, *Body Guards: The Cultural Politics of Gender Ambiguity* London: Routledge.

GATENS, Moira (1991) 'Corporal representation in/and the body politic' in DIPROSE and FERRELL (1991).

GRAY, Stephen (1986) 'A sense of place in the New Literatures in English' in NIGHTINGALE (1986) 5–12.

GROSZ, Elizabeth (1990) 'Inscriptions and body-maps: representations and the corporal' in Threadgold, Terry and Cranny-Francis, Anne (1990) editors, *Feminine Masculine and Representation* Sydney: Allen & Unwin.

HAMMER, Mary (1989a) 'Putting Ireland on the map' *Textual Practice* (Summer) 184–201.

—— (1989b) 'The English look of the Irish map' *Circa* 46 (July/August) 23–5.

HANRAHAN, Johnny (1991) 'Notes on a conversation with Eilis O'Connell, Kathy Prendergast and Vivienne Roche' in *Edge to Edge – Three Sculptors from Ireland* Dublin: Gandon Editions.

HARLEY, J. B. (1988) 'Maps, knowledge and power' in Daniels, Stephen and Cosgrove, Denis (1988) editors, *The Iconography of Landscape: essays in the symbolic representation, design and use of past environments* Cambridge: Cambridge University Press: 277–312.

—— (1992) 'Deconstructing the map' in Barnes, Trevor J. and Duncan, James S. (1992) editors, *Writing Worlds: Discourse, Text and Metaphor in the Representation of Landscape* London: Routledge: 231–47.

HEANEY, Seamus (1980a) *Selected Poems* London: Faber.

—— (1980b) *Preoccupations: Selected Prose 1968–1978* London: Faber.

HILLER, Susan (1991) editor, *The Myth of Primitivism: Perspectives on Art* London: Routledge.

HUGGEN, Graham (1989) 'Decolonising the map; post-colonialism, post-structuralism and the cartographic connection' *Ariel: A Review of International English Literature* Vol. 20, No. 4 (October) 115–31.

KING, Y. (1990) 'Healing the wounds: feminism, ecology and the nature culture dualism' in ORENSTEIN and DIAMOND (1990).

KOLODNY, Annette (1975) *The Lay of the Land: Metaphor as Experience and History in American Life and Letters* Chapel Hill: University of North Carolina Press.

LIVINGSTONE, David N. (1991) 'The moral discourse of climate: historical considerations on race, place and virtue' *Journal of Historical Geography* Vol. 17: 413–34.

—— (1992) '"Never Shall ye Make the Crab Walk Straight": an inquiry into the scientific discourses of racial geography' in DRIVER and ROSE (1992) 37–47.

MAXWELL, Desmond Ernest Stewart (1965) 'Landscape and Theme' in Press, John (1965) editor, *Commonwealth Literature* London: Heinemann: 82–9.

MERCHANT, Carolyn (1990) 'Ecofeminism and feminist theory' in ORENSTEIN and DIAMOND (1990).

MONTROSE, Louis (1991) 'The work of gender in the discourse of discovery' *Representations* Vol 33: 1–41.

MURPHY, Cliona (1989) *The Women's Suffrage Movement and Irish Society in the Early Twentieth Century* New York: Harvester Wheatsheaf.

NASH, Catherine (1993) 'Embodying the nation – the West of Ireland landscape and Irish national identity' in Cronin, Michael and O'Connor, Barbara (1993) editors, *Tourism and Ireland: A Critical Analysis* Cork: Cork University Press.

NIGHTINGALE, Peggy (1986) *A Sense of Place in the New Literatures in English* St Lucia, New York and London: University of Queensland Press.

NORWOOD, Vera and MONK, Janice (1987a) editors, *The Desert is No Lady: Southwestern Landscapes in Women's Writing and Art*, Yale: Yale University Press.

—— (1987b) 'Introduction – perspectives on Gender and Landscape' in NORWOOD and MONK (1987a) 1–9.

O'BRIEN JOHNSON Toni and CAIRNS, David (1991a) editors, *Gender in Irish Writing* Buckingham: Open University Press.

—— (1991b) 'Introduction' in O'BRIEN JOHNSON and CAIRNS (1991).

ORENSTEIN, Gloria and DIAMOND, Irene (1990) editors, *Reweaving the World: The Emergence of Ecofeminism*, San Francisco: Sierra Club.

OWENS, Rosemary Cullen (1984) *Smashing Times: A History of the Irish Woman's Suffrage Movement 1898–1922* Dublin: Attic Press.

PARKER, Andrew, RUSSO, Mary, SOMMER, Doris and YAEGER, Patricia (1992) 'Introduction' in Parker, Andrew, Russo, M, Sommer, Doris and Yaeger, Patricia (1992) editors, *Nationalisms and Sexualities* London: Routledge: 1–18.

PLUMWOOD, Val (1988) 'Woman, humanity and nature' *Radical Philosophy* (Spring) 16–24.

PRENTICE, Chris (1986) 'Rewriting their stories, renaming themselves: post-colonialism and feminism in the fictions of Keri Hulme and Audrey Thomas' *SPAN: Journal of the South Pacific Association for Commonwealth Literature and Language Studies* Vol. 23: 68–80.

RIORDAN, Maurice (1985) 'Eros and history: on contemporary Irish poetry' *The Crane Bag* Vol. 9, No, 1: 49–55.

ROSE, Gillian (1992) 'Geography as a science of observation: the landscape, the gaze and masculinity' in DRIVER and ROSE (1992).

RUDNICK, Lois (1987), 'Re-naming the land – Anglo expatriate women in the southwest' in NORWOOD and MONK (1987a) 10–26.

RUSSELL, George (1912) *Co-operation and Nationality* Dublin: Maunsel.

SLEMON, Stephen (1991) 'Modernism's last post' in ADAM and TIFFIN (1991) 1–9.

SMITH, Paul Julian (1992) *Representing the Other: 'Race', Text and Gender in Spanish and Spanish American Narrative* Oxford: Clarendon Press.

SMYTH, Ailbhe (1991) 'The floozie in the jacuzzi' *Feminist Studies* Vol. 17, No. 1 (Spring) 16–24.

SPIVAK, Gayatri Chakravorty (1992) 'Women in difference: Mahasweta Devi's "Douloti the Bountiful"' in PARKER *et al.* (1992) 96–117.

STEPAN, N. (1985) 'Biological degeneration: races and proper places' in Chamberlain, J. E. and Gilman, S. L. (1985) editors, *Degeneration: The Dark Side of Progress* New York: Columbia University Press.

TAGG, John (1992) *Grounds of Dispute: Art History, Cultural Politics and The Discursive Field* London: Macmillan: 1–39.

TIFFIN, Helen (1986) 'New concepts of person and place in "The Twybon Affair" and "A Bend in the River" in NIGHTINGALE (1986).

—— (1987a) 'Post-colonial literatures and counter-discourse' *Kunapipi* Vol. 9, No. 3: 17–34.

—— (1987b) 'Post-colonialism, post-modernism and the rehabilitation of post-colonial history' *Journal of Commonwealth Literature* Vol. 1: 169–81.

WARD, Margaret (1983) *Unmanageable Revolutionaries: Women and Irish Nationalism* Dingle: Brandon.

WARREN, Karen J. (1987) 'Feminism and ecology: making connections' *Environmental Ethics* Vol. 9: 2–20.

WEEDON, Chris (1987) *Feminist Practice and Poststructuralist Theory* Oxford: Basil Blackwell.

YUVAL-DAVIS, Nira and ANTHIAS, Floya (1989) editors, *Women-Nation-State* New York: St Martin's Press.

EASTER 1991

Máighréad Medbh

I am Ireland and I'm sick
sick in the womb / sick in the head
and I'm sick of lying in this sickbed
and if the medical men don't stop operating /
I'll die

I am Ireland / and if I die
my name will go down in the censor's fire
my face in the mirror is shy /
I have painted it too many times
there's nothing to like about this kind of beauty

Illustration: Marie Leggo

I am Ireland / and I don't know what I am
they tell me things in sham films like The Field /
that the travellers are pink-faced romantics in fairy caravans
that my villages are full of eejits and lúdramáns
that my pagan power is dead
it was made for Hollywood / not for me

I am Ireland / and I'm silenced
I cannot tell my abortions / my divorces / my years of slavery /
my fights for freedom
it's got to the stage I can hardly remember what I had to tell /
and when I do / I speak in whispers

I am Ireland / and I've nowhere to run
I've spent my history / my energy / my power / my money
to build him up /
and he gave me back nothing I didn't take myself

inside my head the facts are loud /
only two women's shelters in Dublin /
on Stephen's Day a man petrol-bombs one /
and on the same day / gets out on bail
abortion is a criminal offence
abortion information is stopped
divorce is denied /
the Gardaí don't interfere
the facts are loud /
Sharon Gregg dies in Mountjoy
Fearghal Carraher dies in Cullyhanna
Patrick Sheehy dies in Nenagh
Dessie Ellis is handed on a stretcher to my enemy /
the facts are loud /
Bishop Cathal Daly wants less talk of AIDS
thousands emigrate each year
half of my children are poor
and the poorest of all are my daughters

I am Ireland / and the poor die young
and the poor are easily sold
and the poor are the ones who fight
and because they fight / they die

I am Ireland / and the Angelus Bell is tolling for me
this illegal border will always be /
unless we get up off our bended knee
the priests run my schools and my history
there's no free state in the Catholic See

I am Ireland / and I'm sick
I'm sick of this tidy house where I exist /
that reminds me of nothing
not of the past / not of the future
I'm sick of depression
I'm sick of shame
I'm sick of poverty
I'm sick of politeness
I'm sick of looking over my shoulder
I'm sick of standing by the shore /
waiting for some prince to come on the tide

Mise Éire /
agus an ghaoth ag éirí láidir i mo chluasa
agus n'fheadar an é biseach nó bás a thiocfaidh

Mise Éire /
agus n'fheadar an bhfuil mé óg nó sean

Mise Éire /
agus níl mé ag feitheamh a thuilleadh

I am Ireland /
and I'm not waiting anymore

Family Feuds: Gender, Nationalism and the Family[1]

Anne McClintock

All nationalisms are gendered, all are invented, and all are dangerous –
dangerous, not in Eric Hobsbawm's sense as having to be opposed, but in
the sense of representing relations to political power and to the
technologies of violence. Nationalism, as Ernest Gellner notes, invents
nations where they do not exist, and most modern nations, despite their
appeal to an august and immemorial past, are of recent invention
(Gellner, 1964). Benedict Anderson warns, however, that Gellner tends
to assimilate 'invention' to 'falsity' rather than to 'imagining' and
'creation'. Anderson, by contrast, views nations as 'imagined communities' in the sense that they are systems of cultural representation
whereby people come to imagine a shared experience of identification
with an extended community (Anderson, 1991: 6). As such, nations are
not simply phantasmagoria of the mind, but are historical and institutional practices through which social difference is invented and
performed. Nationalism becomes, as a result, radically constitutive of
people's identities, through social contests that are frequently violent
and always gendered. But if the invented nature of nationalism has
found wide theoretical currency, explorations of the gendering of the
national imaginary have been conspicuously paltry.

All nations depend on powerful constructions of gender. Despite
nationalisms' ideological investment in the idea of popular *unity*,
nations have historically amounted to the sanctioned institutionalization of gender *difference*. No nation in the world gives women and men
the same access to the rights and resources of the nation-state. Rather
than expressing the flowering into time of the organic essence of a
timeless people, nations are contested systems of cultural representation that limit and legitimize peoples' access to the resources of the
nation-state. Yet with the notable exception of Frantz Fanon, male
theorists have seldom felt moved to explore how nationalism is

implicated in gender power. As a result, as Cynthia Enloe remarks, nationalisms have 'typically sprung from masculinized memory, masculinized humiliation and masculinized hope' (Enloe, 1989: 44).

George Santayana, for one, gives voice to a well-established male view: 'Our nationalism is like our relationship to women: too implicated in our moral nature to be changed honourably, and too accidental to be worth changing'. Santayana's sentence could not be said by a woman, for his 'our' of national agency is male, and his male citizen stands in the same symbolic relation to the nation as a man stands to a woman. Not only are the needs of the nation here identified with the frustrations and aspirations of men, but the representation of male *national* power depends on the prior construction of *gender* difference.

For Gellner, the very definition of nationhood rests on the *male* recognition of identity: 'Men are of the same nation if and only if they recognize each other as being from the same nation.' (Gellner, 1964) For Etienne Balibar, such recognition aligns itself inevitably with the notion of a 'race' structured about the transmission of male power and property: 'Ultimately the nation must align itself, spiritually as well as physically or carnally, with the "race", the *"patrimony"* to be protected from all degradation' (Balibar, 1991, my emphasis). Even Fanon, who at other moments knew better, writes 'The look that the native turns on the settler town is a look of lust . . . to sit at the settler's table, to sleep in the settler's bed, with his wife if possible. The colonized man is an envious man' (Fanon, 1963: 30). For Fanon, both colonizer and colonized are here unthinkingly male, and the manichaean agon of decolonization is waged over the territoriality of female, domestic space.

All too often in male nationalisms, *gender* difference between women and men serves to symbolically define the limits of *national* difference and power between *men*. Excluded from direct action as national citizens, women are subsumed symbolically into the national body politic as its boundary and metaphoric limit: 'Singapore girl, you're a great way to fly.' Women are typically construed as the symbolic bearers of the nation, but are denied any direct relation to national agency. As Elleke Boehmer notes in her fine essay, the 'motherland' of male nationalism may thus 'not signify "home" and "source" to women' (Boehmer, 1991: 5). Boehmer notes that the male role in the nationalist scenario is typically 'metonymic', that is, men are contiguous with each other and with the national whole. Women, by contrast, appear 'in a metaphoric or symbolic role' (Boehmer, 1991: 6). In an important intervention, Nira Yuval-Davis and Floya Anthias thus identify five major ways in which women have been implicated in nationalism (Yuval-Davis and Anthias, 1989: 7):

- as biological reproducers of the members of national collectivities
- as reproducers of the boundaries of national groups (through restrictions on sexual or marital relations)
- as active transmitters and producers of the national culture

• as symbolic signifiers of national difference
• as active participants in national struggles

Nationalism is thus constituted from the very beginning as a gendered discourse, and cannot be understood without a theory of gender power. None the less, theories of nationalism reveal a double disavowal. If male theorists are typically indifferent to the gendering of nations, feminist analyses of nationalism have been lamentably few and far between. White feminists, in particular, have been slow to recognize nationalism as a feminist issue. In much Western, socialist feminism, as Yuval-Davis and Anthias point out, '[i]ssues of ethnicity and nationality have tended to be ignored.'

A feminist theory of nationalism might be strategically fourfold: investigating the gendered formation of sanctioned male theories; bringing into historical visibility women's active cultural and political participation in national formations; bringing nationalist institutions into critical relation with other social structures and institutions, while at the same time paying scrupulous attention to the structures of racial, ethnic and class power that continue to bedevil privileged forms of feminism.

The national family of man

A paradox lies at the heart of most national narratives. Nations are frequently figured through the iconography of familial and domestic space. The term 'nation' derives from 'natio': to be born. We speak of nations as 'motherlands' and 'fatherlands'. Foreigners 'adopt' countries that are not their native homes, and are 'naturalized' into the national family. We talk of the Family of Nations, of 'homelands' and 'native' lands. In Britain, immigration matters are dealt with at the Home Office; in the United States, the President and his wife are called the First Family. Winnie Mandela was, until her recent fall from grace, honoured as South Africa's 'Mother of the Nation'. In this way, nations are symbolically figured as *domestic genealogies*. Yet, at the same time, since the mid nineteenth century in the West, 'the family' itself has been figured as the *antithesis* of history.

The family trope is important in at least two ways. First, the family offers a 'natural' figure for sanctioning social *hierarchy* within a putative organic *unity* of interests. Second, it offers a 'natural' trope for figuring historical *time*. After 1859 and the advent of social Darwinism, Britain's emergent national narrative took increasing shape around the image of the evolutionary Family of Man. The 'family' offered an indispensable metaphoric figure by which hierarchical (and, one might add, often contradictory) social distinctions could be shaped into a single *historical* genesis narrative. Yet a curious paradox emerges. The family as a metaphor offered a single genesis narrative for national history, while, at the same time, the family as an *institution* became voided of history. As the nineteenth century drew on, the family as an institution was figured as existing, by natural decree, beyond the commodity market, beyond politics, and beyond history proper. (Davidoff, L. and Hall, C, 1987) The family thus became, at one and the same time, both the organizing figure for national *history*, as well as its *antithesis*.

Edward Said has pointed to a transition in the late Victorian upper middle class from a culture of 'filiation' (familial relations) to a culture of 'affiliation' (non-familial relations). Said argues that a perceived crisis in the late Victorian upper-middle-class family took on the aspect of a pervasive cultural affliction. The decay of filiation was, he argues, typically attended by a second moment – the turn to a compensatory order of affiliation, which might variously be an institution, a vision, a credo, or a vocation. While retaining the powerful distinction between filiation and affiliation, I wish to complicate the linear thrust of Said's story. In the course of the nineteenth century, the social function of the great service families (which had been invested in filiative rituals of patrilineal rank and subordination) became displaced on to the national bureaucracy. So, too, the filiative image of the family was projected on to emerging affiliative institutions as their shadowy, naturalized form. Thus, I argue, the filiative order did not disappear: rather it flourished as a metaphoric after-image, reinvented within the new orders of the nation-state, the industrial bureaucracy, and imperial capitalism. Increasingly, filiation took an imperial shape, as the cultural invention of the evolutionary Family of Man was projected both on to the national metropolis and the colonial bureaucracy as its natural, legitimizing shape.

The significance of the family trope was twofold. First, the family offered an indispensable figure for sanctioning social *hierarchy* within a putative *organic unity* of interests. Since the subordination of woman to man, and child to adult, was deemed a natural fact, other forms of social hierarchy could be depicted in familial terms to guarantee social difference as a category of nature. The family image was thus drawn on to figure *hierarchy within unity* as an 'organic' element of historical progress, and thereby became indispensable for legitimizing exclusion and hierarchy within non-familial (affiliative) social formations such as nationalism, liberal individualism and imperialism. The metaphoric depiction of social hierarchy as natural and familial – the 'national family', the global 'family of nations', the colony as a 'family of black children ruled over by a white father' – thus depended on the prior naturalizing of the social subordination of women and children within the domestic sphere.

Secondly, the family offered an indispensable trope for figuring what was often violent, *historical change* as natural, *organic time*. Since children 'naturally' progress into adults, projecting the family image on to national and imperial 'Progress' enabled what was often murderously violent change to be legitimized as the progressive unfolding of natural decree. National or imperial intervention could be figured as an organic, non-revolutionary progression that naturally contained hierarchy within unity: paternal fathers ruling benignly over immature children.

The evolutionary family thus captured, in one potent trope, the idea of *social discontinuity* (hierarchy through space) and temporal *discontinuity* (hierarchy across time) as a natural, *organic continuity*. The idea of the Family of Man became invaluable in its capacity to give state and imperial intervention the alibi of nature.

As Fanon eloquently describes it in 'Algeria unveiled', imperial intervention frequently took shape as a domestic rescue drama. 'Around the family life of the Algerian, the occupier piled up a whole mass of judgements . . . thus attempting to confine the Algerian within a circle of guilt' (Fanon, 1965: 38). The dream of the 'total domestication of Algerian society' came to haunt colonial authority, and the domesticated, female body became the terrain over which the military contest was fought.

In modern Europe, citizenship is the legal representation of a person's relationship to the rights and resources of the nation-state. But the putatively universalist concept of national citizenship becomes unstable when seen from the position of women. In post-French Revolution Europe, women were not incorporated directly into the nation-state as citizens, but only indirectly through men, as dependent members of the family in private and public law. The Code Napoleon was the first modern statute to decree that the wife's nationality should follow her husband's, an example other European countries briskly followed. A woman's *political* relation to the nation was submerged as a *social* relation to a man through marriage. For women, citizenship in the nation was mediated by the marriage relation within the family.

The gendering of nation time

A number of critics have followed Tom Nairn in naming the nation 'the modern Janus' (Nairn, 1977). For Nairn, the nation takes shape as a contradictory figure of time: one face gazing back into the primordial mists of the past, the other into an infinite future. Deniz Kandiyoti expresses the temporal contradiction with clarity: '[Nationalism] presents itself both as a modern project that melts and transforms traditional attachments in favour of new identities *and* as a reflection of authentic cultural values culled from the depths of a presumed communal past' [Kandiyoti, 1992). Bhabha, following Nairn and Anderson, writes: 'Nations, like narratives, lose their origins in the myths of time and only fully realize their horizons in the mind's eye' (Bhabha, 1991: 1). Bhabha and Anderson borrow here on Walter Benjamin's crucial insight into the temporal paradox of modernity. For Benjamin, a central feature of nineteenth century industrial capitalism was the 'use of archaic images to identify what was historically new about the "nature" of commodities' (Buck-Morss, 1989: 67). In Benjamin's insight, the mapping of 'Progress' depends on systematically *inventing* images of 'archaic' time to identify what is historically 'new' about enlightened, national progress. Anderson can thus ask: 'Supposing "antiquity" were,

at a certain historical juncture, the *necessary consequence* of "novelty"?'
(Anderson, 1991: xiv).

What is less often noticed, however, is that the temporal anomaly
within nationalism – veering between nostalgia for the past, and the
impatient, progressive sloughing off of the past – is typically resolved by
figuring the contradiction as a 'natural' division of *gender*. Women are
represented as the atavistic and authentic 'body' of national tradition
(inert, backward-looking, and natural), embodying nationalism's conservative principle of continuity. Men, by contrast, represent the
progressive agent of national modernity (forward-thrusting, potent and
historic), embodying nationalism's progressive, or revolutionary principle of discontinuity. Nationalism's anomalous relation to *time* is thus
managed as a natural relation to *gender*.

Johannes Fabian's important meditation on time and anthropology, *Time and the Other* (1983), shows how, following Darwin, the
social evolutionists broke the hold of biblical chronology (chronicle time)
by secularizing time and placing it at the disposal of the empirical,
imperial project (chronological time). In order to do this, Fabian points
out, 'they spatialized time'. With the publication of *The Origin of
Species*, Charles Darwin bestowed on the developing global project of
empiricism a decisive dimension – secular Time as the agent of a unified
world history. The axis of *time* was projected on to the axis of *space*, and
history became global. Now not only natural space, but also historical
time, could be collected and mapped on to a global, taxonomic science of
the surface. Most importantly, history, especially national and imperial
history, took on the character of a spectacle.

The exemplary figure for spatializing time was the Family Tree.
The social evolutionists took the ancient image of the divine, cosmologi-
cal Tree and secularized it as a natural genealogy of global, imperial
history. In the secularized Tree of Time, three principles emerge.
Mapped against the global Tree, the world's discontinuous 'nations'
appear to be marshalled within a single, hierarchical European ur-
narrative. Second, history is imaged as naturally teleological, an
organic process of upward growth, with the European nation as the
apogee of progress. Third, inconvenient discontinuities are ranked and
subordinated into a hierarchical structure of branching time – the
differential progress of 'racially' different nations mapped against the
tree's self-evident boughs, with 'lesser nations' destined, by nature, to
perch on its lower branches.

Time, however, was thus not only *secularized*, it was *domesticated*,
a point Fabian, for one, does not address. Social evolutionism and
anthropology gave to national politics a concept of natural time as
familial. In the image of the Family Tree, evolutionary 'progress' was
represented as a series of anatomically distinct 'family' types, organized
into a linear procession. Violent national and imperial change thus took
on the character of an evolving spectacle, under the organizing rubric of
the family. The merging of the 'racial' evolutionary Tree and the
'gendered' Family into the Family Tree of Man provided scientific

racism with a simultaneously gendered and racial image through which it could popularize the idea of imperial Progress.

Britain's emerging national narrative gendered time by figuring women (like the colonized and the working class) as inherently atavistic – the conservative repository of the national archaic. Women, it was argued, did not inhabit history proper, but existed, like colonized peoples, in a permanently anterior time within the modern nation, as anachronistic humans, childlike, irrational and regressive – the living archive of the national archaic. White, middle-class men, by contrast, were seen to embody the forward-thrusting agency of national 'progress'. Thus the figure of the national Family of Man reveals a persistent paradox. National 'Progress' (conventionally, the invented domain of male, public space) was figured as *familial*, while the family itself (conventionally, the domain of private, female space) was figured as *beyond history*. With these theoretical remarks in mind, I wish now to turn to the paradoxical relation between the invented constructions of family and nation, as they have taken shape within South Africa in both black and white women's contradictory relations to the competing national genealogies.

One can safely say, at this point, that there is no single narrative of the nation. Different genders, classes, ethnicities and generations do not identify with, or experience the myriad national formations in the same way; nationalisms are invented, performed and consumed in ways that do not follow a universal blueprint. At the very least, the breathtaking Eurocentricism of Hobsbawm's dismissal of Third World nationalisms warrants sustained criticism. In a gesture of sweeping condescension, Hobsbawm nominates Europe as nationalism's 'original home', while 'all the anti-imperial movements of any significance' are unceremoniously dumped into three categories: mimicry of Europe, anti-Western xenophobia, and the 'natural high spirits of martial tribes' (Hobsbawm, 1990: 151). A feminist investigation of national difference might, by contrast, take into account the dynamic social and historic contexts of national struggles, their strategic mobilizing of popular forces, their myriad, varied trajectories, and their relation to other social institutions. We might do well to develop a more theoretically complex, and strategically subtle *genealogy* of nationalisms. In South Africa, certainly, the competing Afrikaner and African nationalisms have had both distinct and overlapping trajectories, with very different consequences for women.

Afrikaner nationalism and gender

Until the 1860s, Britain had scant interest in its unpromising colony at the southern tip of Africa. Only upon the discovery of diamonds (1867) and gold (1886) were the Union Jack and the redcoats shipped out with any real sense of imperial mission. But very quickly, mining needs for cheap labour and a centralized state collided with traditional farming interests, and out of these contradictions, in the conflict for control over African land and labour, exploded the Anglo-Boer War of 1899–1902.

Afrikaner nationalism was a doctrine of crisis. After their defeat by the British, the bloodied remnants of the scattered Boer communities had to forge a new counter-culture if they were to survive in the emergent capitalist state. From the outset, the invention of this counter-culture had a clear *class* component. When the Boer generals and the British capitalists swore blood-brotherhood in the Union of 1910, the rag-tag legion of 'poor whites' with little or no prospects, the modest clerks and shopkeepers, the small farmers and poor teachers, the intellectuals and petite bourgeoisie, all precarious in the new state, began to identify themselves as the vanguard of a new Afrikanerdom, the chosen emissaries of the national *volk* (Moodie, 1975; O'Meara, 1983).

To begin with, however, Afrikaners had no monolithic identity, no common historic purpose, and no single unifying language. They were a disunited, scattered people, speaking a medley of High Dutch and local dialects, with smatterings of the slave, Nguni and Khoisan languages – scorned as the '*kombuistaal*' (kitchen-language) of house-servants, slaves and women. Afrikaners therefore had, quite literally, to invent themselves. The new, invented community of the *volk* required the conscious creation of a single print-language, a popular press and a literate populace. At the same time, the invention of tradition required a class of cultural brokers and image-makers to do the inventing. The 'language movement' of the early twentieth century, in the flurry of poems, magazines, newspapers, novels and countless cultural events, provided just such a movement, fashioning the myriad Boer vernaculars into a single identifiable Afrikaans language. In the early decades of the twentieth century, as Isabel Hofmeyr has brilliantly shown, an elaborate labour of 'regeneration' was undertaken, as the despised '*Hotnotstaal*' ('Hottentot's language') was revamped and purged of its rural, "degenerate" associations, and elevated to the status of the august 'mother tongue' of the Afrikaans people (Hofmeyr, 1987: 97). In 1918, Afrikaans was legally recognized as a language.

At the same time, the invention of Afrikaner tradition had a clear *gender* component. In 1918, a small, clandestine clique of Afrikaans men launched a secret society, with the express mission of capturing the loyalties of dispirited Afrikaners and fostering white male business power. The tiny white brotherhood swiftly burgeoned into a secret, country-wide mafia that came to exert enormous power over all aspects of Nationalist policy (Moodie, 1975; O'Meara, 1983). The gender bias of the society, as of Afrikanerdom as a whole, is neatly summed up in its name: the Broederbond (the brotherhood). Henceforth, Afrikaner nationalism would be synonymous with white male interests, white male aspirations and white male politics. Indeed, in a recent effort to shore up its waning power, the Broederbond is currently debating whether to admit so-called 'Coloured' Afrikaans speaking men into the brotherhood. All women will, however, continue to be barred.

In the voluminous Afrikaner historiography, the history of the *volk* is organized around a male national narrative figured as an imperial journey into empty lands. The journey proceeds forwards in *geographical* space, but backwards in *racial* and *gender* time, to what is figured as a prehistoric zone of linguistic, racial and gender 'degeneration'. The myth of the 'empty land' is simultaneously the myth of the 'virgin land' – effecting a double erasure. Within the colonial narrative, to be 'virgin' is to be empty of desire, voided of sexual agency, and passively awaiting the thrusting, male insemination of European military history, language and 'reason'. The feminizing of 'virgin' colonial lands also effects a territorial appropriation, for if the land is virgin, Africans cannot claim aboriginal territorial rights, and the white male patrimony can be violently assured.

At the heart of the continent, an historic agon is staged, as 'degenerate' Africans 'falsely' claim entitlement to the land. A divinely organized military conflict baptizes the nation in a male birthing ritual, which grants to white men the patrimony of land and history. The nation emerges as the progeny of male history through the motor of military might. At the centre of this imperial gospel, stands the contradictory figure of the *volksmoeder*, the mother of the nation.

The central emblem of Afrikaans historiography is the Great Trek, and each trek is figured as a family presided over by a single, epic male patriarch. In 1938, two decades after the recognition of Afrikaans as a language, an epic extravaganza of invented tradition enflamed Afrikanerdom into a delirium of nationalist passion. Dubbed the *Tweede Trek* (Second Trek), or the *Eeufees* (Centenary), the event celebrated the Boers' first mutinous Great Trek in 1838 away from British laws and the effrontery of slave emancipation. The Centenary also commemorated the Boer massacre of the Zulus at the Battle of Blood River. Nine replicas of Voortrekker wagons were built – the reinvention of the archaic to sanction modernity. Each wagon was literally baptized, and named after a male Voortrekker hero. No wagon was named after an adult woman. One was, however, called generically, *Vrou en Moeder* (wife and mother). This wagon, creaking across the country, symbolized woman's relation to the nation as indirect, mediated through her social relation to men, her national identity lying in her unpaid services and sacrifices, through husband and family, to the *volk*. Each wagon became the microcosm of colonial society at large: the whip-wielding white patriarch prancing on horseback, black servants toiling alongside, white mother and children sequestered in the wagon – the women's starched white bonnets signifying the purity of the race, the decorous surrender of their sexuality to the patriarch, and the invisibility of white female labour.

The wagons rumbled along different routes from Cape Town to Pretoria, sparking along the way an orgy of national pageantry, and engulfing the country in a four-month spectacle of invented tradition. Along the way, white men grew beards and white women donned the ancestral bonnets. Huge crowds gathered to greet the wagons. As the

Women as Boundary Markers of the Afrikaans Nation

trekkers passed through the towns, babies were named after trekker heroes, as were roads and public buildings. Not a few girls were baptized with the improbable but popular favourite: Eeufesia (Centeneria). The affair climaxed in Pretoria in a spectacular marathon, with explicit Third Reich overtones, led by thousands of Afrikaner boy scouts bearing flaming torches.

The first point about the *Tweede Trek* is that it invented white nationalist traditions and celebrated unity where none had existed before, creating the illusion of a collective identity through the political staging of vicarious *spectacle*. The second point is that the Nationalists adopted this ploy from the Nazis. The Tweede Trek was inspired not only by the Nazi creed of *Blut und Boden*, but a new *political style*: the Nuremberg politics of fetish symbol and cultural persuasion.

In our time, I suggest, national collectivity is experienced pre-eminently through spectacle. Here I depart from Anderson, who sees nationalism as emerging primarily from the Gutenberg technology of print capitalism. Anderson neglects the fact that print capital has, until recently, been accessible to a relatively small literate élite. One could argue that the singular power of nationalism has been its capacity to organize a sense of popular, collective unity through the management of mass national *commodity spectacle*.

In this respect, nationalism inhabits the realm of fetishism. Despite the commitment of European nationalism (following Hegel) to the idea of the nation-state as the embodiment of rational Progress, nationalism has been experienced and transmitted primarily through fetishism – precisely the cultural form that the Enlightenment denigrated as the antithesis of 'Reason'. More often than not, nationalism takes shape through the visible, ritual organization of fetish objects: flags, uniforms, airplane logos, maps, anthems, national flowers, national cuisines and architectures, as well as through the organization of collective fetish spectacle – in team sports, military displays, mass rallies, the myriad forms of popular culture, and so on. Far from being purely sexual icons, fetishes embody crises in social value, which are projected on to and embodied in impassioned objects.[2] Considerable work remains to be done on the ways in which women consume, refuse or negotiate the male fetish rituals of national spectacle.

The *Eeufees* was, by anyone's standards, a triumph of image management, complete with the spectacular regalia of flags, flaming torches, patriotic songs, incendiary speeches, costumes and crowd management. More than anything, the *Eeufees* revealed the extent to which nationalism is a symbolic *performance* of invented community: the *Eeufees* was a calculated and self-conscious effort by the Broeder-bond to paper over the myriad regional, gender and class tensions that threatened them. As a fetishistic displacement of difference, it suc-ceeded famously, for the success of the *Tweede Trek* in mobilizing a sense of white Afrikaner collectivity was a major reason, though certainly not the only one, for the Nationalists' triumphant sweep to power in 1948.[3]

From the outset, as the *Eeufees* bore witness, Afrikaner national-ism was dependent not only on powerful constructions of racial difference, but also on powerful constructions of gender difference. A gendered division of national creation prevailed, whereby men were seen to embody the political and economic agency of the *volk*, while women were the (unpaid) keepers of tradition and the *volk's* moral and spiritual mission. This gendered division of labour is summed up in the colonial gospel of the family, and the presiding icon of the *volksmoeder* (the mother of the nation). The *volksmoeder*, however, is less a biological fact than a social category. Nor is it an ideology imposed willy-nilly on hapless female victims. Rather, it is a changing, dynamic ideology rife with paradox, under constant contest by men and women, and adapted constantly to the pressures arising from African resistance and the conflict between Afrikaner colonialists and British imperialists.

The invention of the *volksmoeder*: mum's the word

The Anglo-Boer War (fundamentally a war over African land and labour) was in many respects waged as a war on Boer women. In an effort to break Boer resistance, the British torched the farms and lands, and herded thousands of women and children into concentration camps, where 25,000 women and children perished of hunger, desolation and disease. Yet, after the Anglo-Boer War, the political power of the fierce Boer women was muted and transformed. In 1913, three years after Union, the *Vrouemonument* (Women's Monument) was erected in homage to the female victims of the war. The monument took the form of a circular, domestic enclosure, where women stand weeping with their children. Here, women's martial role as fighters and farmers was purged of its indecorously militant potential, and replaced by the figure of the lamenting mother with babe in arms. The monument enshrined Afrikaner womanhood as neither militant nor political, but as suffering, stoical and self-sacrificial (Brink, 1990). Women's disempowerment was figured not as expressive of the politics of gender difference, stemming from colonial women's ambiguous relation to imperial domination, but as emblematic of national (that is, male) disempowerment. By portraying the Afrikaner *nation* symbolically as a weeping *woman*, the mighty male embarrassment of military defeat could be overlooked, and the memory of women's vital efforts during the war washed away in images of feminine tears and maternal loss.

The icon of the *volksmoeder* is paradoxical. On the one hand, it recognizes the power of (white) motherhood; on the other hand, it is a retrospective iconography of gender containment, containing women's mutinous power within an iconography of domestic service. Defined as weeping victims of African menace, white women's activism is overlooked and their disempowerment thereby ratified.

Indeed, in the early decades of this century, as Hofmeyr shows, women played a crucial role in the invention of Afrikanerdom. The family household was seen as the last bastion beyond British control, and the cultural power of Afrikaner motherhood was mobilized in the service of white nation-building. Afrikaans was a language fashioned very profoundly by women's labours, within the economy of the domestic household. 'Not for nothing' as Hofmeyr notes, 'was it called the "mother tongue".' (1987)

In Afrikaner nationalism, motherhood is a political concept under constant contest. It is important to emphasize this for two reasons. Erasing Afrikaner women's historic agency also erases their historic complicity in the annals of apartheid. White women were not the weeping bystanders of apartheid history, but active, if decidedly disempowered, participants in the invention of Afrikaner identity. As such they were complicit in deploying the power of motherhood in the exercise and legitimation of white domination. Certainly, white women were jealously and brutally denied any formal political power, but were compensated by their limited authority in the household. Clutching this small power, they became complicit in the racism that suffuses Afrikaner nationalism. For this reason, black South African women have been justly suspicious of any easy assumption of a universal, essential sisterhood in suffering. White women are both colonized and colonizers, ambiguously implicated in the history of African dispossession.

Gender and the ANC: 'No longer in a future heaven'

African nationalism has roughly the same historic vintage as Afrikaner nationalism. Forged in the crucible of imperial thuggery, mining capitalism and rapid industrialization, African nationalism was, like its Afrikaner counterpart, the product of conscious reinvention, the enactment of a new political collectivity by specific cultural and political agents. But its racial and gender components were very different, and African nationalism would describe its own distinct trajectory across the century.

In 1910 the Union of South Africa was formed, uniting the four squabbling provinces under a single legislature. Yet at the 'national' convention, not a single black South African was present. For Africans the Union was an act of profound betrayal. A colour bar banished Africans from skilled labour, and the franchise was denied to all but a handful. And so, in 1912, African men descended on Bloemfontein from all over South Africa to protest a Union in which no black person had a voice. At this gathering, the South African Natives National Congress was launched, soon to become the African National Congress.

At the outset, the ANC, like Afrikaner nationalism, had a narrow class base. Drawn from the tiny urban intelligentsia and petite bourgeoisie, its members were mostly mission-educated teachers and clerks, small businessmen and traders, the kind of men whom Fanon described as 'dusted over with colonial culture'. They were urban, anti-tribal and assimilationist, demanding full civic participation in the great British Empire, rather than confrontation and radical change. They were also solidly male (Lodge, 1991).

For the first thirty years of the ANC, black women's relation to nationalism was structured around a contradiction: their exclusion from full political membership within the ANC contrasted with their increasing grass-roots activism. As Frene Ginwala (1990) has argued, women's resistance was shaped from below. While the language of the ANC was the *inclusive* language of national unity, the Congress was in fact *exclusive* and hierarchical, ranked by an upper house of chiefs (which protected traditional patriarchal authority through descent), a lower house of elected representatives (all male), and an executive (all male). Indians and so-called 'coloureds' were excluded from full membership. Wives of male members could join as 'auxiliary members', but were denied formal political representation, as well as the power to vote. Their subordinate, service role to nationalism was summed up in the draft constitution of the SANNC (later the ANC), which saw women's political role within nationalism as mediated by the marriage relation, and as replicating wives' domestic roles within marriage: 'All the wives of the members ... shall ipso facto become auxiliary members. ... It shall be the duty of all auxiliary members to provide suitable shelter and entertainment for delegates to the Congress.'

In 1913 the white state saw fit to impose passes on women in an effort to pre-empt their migration to the cities. In outraged response, hundreds of women marched mutinously on Bloemfontein to fling back their passes, and for their temerity met the full brunt of state wrath in a barrage of arrests, imprisonment and hard labour. Women's insurgence alarmed both the state and not a few African men. None the less, the climate of militancy gave birth to the Bantu Women's League of the African National Congress, which was launched in 1918, drawing by and large, but not solely, on the tiny, educated, Christian élite. Thus from the outset, women's organized participation in African national-ism stemmed less from the invitation of men, than from their own politicization in resisting the violence of state decree. At this time, however, women's potential militancy was muted, and their political agency domesticated by the language of familial service and subordi-nation. Women's volunteer work was approved in so far as it served the interests of the (male) 'nation', and women's political identity was figured as merely supportive and auxiliary. As President Seme said: 'No national movement can be strong unless the women volunteers come forward and offer their services to the nation.'[4] At women's own insistence, the ANC granted women full membership and voting rights in 1943. It had taken thirty-one years. None the less, women's national mission was still trivialized and domesticated, defined as providing 'suitable shelter and entertainment for members or delegates.'[5]

After the Urban Areas Act of 1937, which severely curtailed women's movements, new insistence began to be voiced for a more militant and explicitly political national women's organization: 'We women can no longer remain in the background or concern ourselves only with domestic and sports affairs. The time has arrived for women to enter the political field and stand shoulder to shoulder with their men in the struggle.' (Mpama, 1937) In 1943, the ANC decided that a Women's League be formed, yet tensions would persist between women's calls for greater autonomy, and men's anxieties about losing control.

During the turbulent fifties, however, the ANC Women's League thrived. This was the decade of the Defiance Campaign, the Freedom Charter, the Congress Alliance, and the Federation of South African Women. In 1956 thousands of women marched on Pretoria to once more protest against passes for women, and the Women's Charter was formed, calling for land redistribution, for worker benefits and union rights, housing and food subsidies, the abolition of child labour, universal education, the right to vote, and equal rights with men in property, marriage and child custody. It is seldom noted, however, that this charter preceded the Freedom Charter, and inspired much of its substance.

Within African nationalism, as in its Afrikaans counterpart, women's political agency has been couched in the presiding ideology of motherhood. Winnie Mandela has long been hailed as 'Mother of the Nation', and Miriam Makeba, the singer, is reverently addressed as 'Ma Africa'.[6] Motherhood, however, is less the universal and biological quintessence of womanhood, than it is a social category under constant contest. African women have embraced, transmuted and transformed

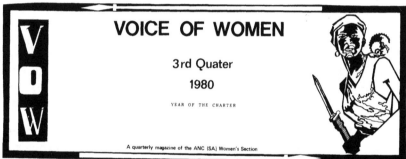

the ideology in a variety of ways, working strategically within traditional ideology to justify untraditional public militancy. Unlike
Afrikaans women, moreover, African women appealed to a racially
inclusive image of motherhood in their campaigns to fashion a non-
racial alliance with white women. A Federation of South African
Women pamphlet of 1958 exhorted white women: 'In the name of
humanity, can you as a woman, as a mother, tolerate this?' In 1986
Albertina Sisulu appealed impatiently to white women: 'A mother is a
mother, black or white. Stand up and be counted with other women.'

Over the decades, African women nationalists, unlike their Afrikaans counterparts, have transformed and infused the ideology of
motherhood with an increasingly insurrectionary cast, identifying
themselves more and more as the 'mothers of revolution'. Since the
seventies, women's local rites of defiance have been mirrored on a
national scale in rents and bus boycotts, organized squatter camps,
strikes, anti-rape protests, and community activism of myriad kinds.
Even under the State of Emergency, women have everywhere enlarged
their militancy, insisting not only on their right to political agency, but
also on their right of access to the technologies of violence.[7]

Black women's relation to nationalism has thus undergone significant historical changes over the years. At the outset, women were

denied formal representation, then their volunteer work was put at the service of the national revolution, still largely male. Gradually, as a result of women's own insurrections, the need for women's full partici- pation in the national liberation movement was granted, but their emancipation was still figured as the handmaiden of national revol- ution. Only recently has women's empowerment been recognized in its own right, distinct from the national, democratic and socialist revol- ution. None the less, the degree to which this rhetorical recognition will find political and institutional form remains to be seen.

Feminism and nationalism

For many decades, African women have been loath to talk of women's emancipation outside the terms of the national liberation movement.[8] During the sixties and seventies, black women were understandably wary of the middle-class feminism that was sputtering fitfully to life in the white universities and suburbs. African women raised justifiably sceptical eyebrows at a white feminism that vaunted itself as giving tongue to a universal sisterhood in suffering. At the same time, women's position within the nationalist movement was still precarious, and women could ill afford to antagonize men so embattled, and already so reluctant to surrender whatever patriarchal power they still enjoyed.

In recent years, however, a transformed African discourse on feminism has emerged, with black women demanding the right to fashion the terms of nationalist feminism to meet their own needs and situations.[9] On 2 May 1990, the National Executive of the ANC issued an historic 'Statement on the Emancipation of Women', which forth- rightly proclaimed: 'The experience of other societies has shown that the emancipation of women is not a by-product of a struggle for democracy, national liberation or socialism. It has to be addressed within our own organization, the mass democratic movement and in the society as a whole.' The document is unprecedented in placing South African women's resistance in an international context, in granting feminism independent historic agency, and in declaring, into the bargain, that all 'laws, customs, traditions and practices which discriminate against women shall be held to be unconstitutional.' If the ANC remains faithful to this document, virtually all existing practises in South Africa's legal, political and social life will be rendered unconstitutional.

A few months later, on 17 June 1990, the leadership of the ANC Women's Section, recently returned to South Africa from exile, insisted on the strategic validity of the term 'feminism': 'Feminism has been misinterpreted in most third world countries . . . there is nothing wrong with feminism. It is as progressive or reactionary as nationalism. Nationalism can be reactionary or progressive. We have not got rid of the term nationalism. And with feminism it is the same.' Rather, feminism should be tailored to meet local needs and concerns.

Yet very real uncertainties for women remain. So far, theoretical and strategic analyses of South Africa's gender imbalances have not run deep. There has been little strategic rethinking of how, in particular, to transform labour relations within the household, and women are not given the same political visibility as men. At a recent COSATU (Congress of South African Trade Unions) convention, trade union women called for attention to sexual harassment in the unions, but their demand was brusquely flicked aside by male unionists as a decadent symptom of 'bourgeois imperialist feminism'. Lesbian and gay activists have been similarly condemned as supporting lifestyles that are no more than invidious imports of empire.

There is not only one feminism, nor is there one patriarchy. Feminism, like nationalism, is not transhistorical. Feminism is imperialist when it puts the interests and needs of privileged women in imperialist countries above the local needs of disempowered women and men, borrowing from patriarchal privilege. In the last decade, women of colour have been vehement in challenging privileged feminists whose racial and class power seems invisible to them. In an important article, Chandra Talpade Mohanty (Mohanty, 1991) challenges the appropriation of women of colour's struggles by white women, specifically through the use of the category 'Third World Woman' as a singular, monolithic, and paradigmatically victimized subject.

Denouncing all feminisms as imperialist, however, erases from memory the long histories of women's resistance to local and imperialist patriarchies. As Kumari Jayawardena notes (Jayawardena, 1986), many women's mutinies around the world predated Western feminism, or occurred without any contact with Western feminists. Moreover, if all feminisms are derided as a pathology of the West, there is a very real danger that Western, white feminists will remain hegemonic, for the simple reason that such women have comparatively privileged access to publishing, the international media, education and money. A good deal of this feminism may well be inappropriate to women living under very different situations. Instead, women of colour are calling for the right to fashion feminism to suit their own worlds. The singular contribution of nationalist feminism has been its insistence on relating feminist struggles to other liberation movements.

All too frequently, male nationalists have condemned feminism as divisive, bidding women hold their tongues until after the revolution. Yet feminism is a political response to gender conflict, not its cause. To insist on silence about gender conflict when it already exists, is to cover over, and thereby ratify, women's disempowerment. To ask women to wait until after the revolution, serves merely as a strategic tactic to defer women's demands. Not only does it conceal the fact that nationalisms are from the outset constituted in gender power, but, as the lessons of international history portend, women who are not empowered to organize during the struggle will not be empowered to organize after the struggle. If nationalism is not transformed by an analysis of gender power, the nation-state will remain a repository of male hopes, male aspirations and male privilege.

All too often, the doors of tradition are slammed in women's faces. Yet traditions are both the outcome and the record of past political contests, as well as the sites of present contest. In a nationalist revolution, both women and men should be empowered to decide which traditions are outmoded, which should be transformed, and which should be preserved. Male nationalists frequently argue that colonialism or capitalism has been women's ruin, with patriarchy merely a nasty second cousin destined to wither away when the real villain finally expires. Yet nowhere has a national or socialist revolution brought a full feminist revolution in its train. In many nationalist or socialist countries women's concerns are at best paid lip service, at worst greeted with hilarity. If women have come to do men's work, men have not come to share women's work. Nowhere has feminism in its own right been allowed to be more than the maidservant to nationalism. A crucial question remains for progressive nationalism: can the iconography of the family be retained as the figure for national unity, or must an alternative, radical iconography be developed?

Frantz Fanon's prescient warnings against the pitfalls of the national consciousness were never more urgent than now. For Fanon, nationalism gives vital expression to popular memory and is strategically essential for mobilizing the national populace. At the same time, no one was more aware than Fanon of the attendant risks of projecting a fetishistic denial of difference on to a conveniently abstracted 'collective will'. In South Africa, to borrow Fanon's phrase, national transformation is 'no longer in a future heaven'. Yet the current situation gives sober poignancy, especially for women, to the lines from Pontecorvo's famous film on the Algerian national war of liberation, *The Battle of Algiers*: 'It is difficult to start a revolution, more difficult to sustain it. But it's later, when we've won, that the real difficulties will begin.'

Notes

Anne McClintock is an associate professor at Columbia University, where she teaches gender and cultural studies. She is currently researching nationalism and gender in South Africa on an SSRC-MacArthur International Peace and Security Fellowship. Her book *Maids, Maps and Mines: Gender and Imperialism* is coming out in 1993.

1 Parts of this paper appeared in 'No Longer in a Future Heaven', (1991) *TRANSITION* 51, 104–23.
2 I critique the Freudian/Lacanian theory of fetishism in 'The return of female fetishism and the fiction of the phallus', in *New Formations* Spring 1992. I expand on the fetishistic nature of national spectacle in my book, *Maids, Maps and Mines: Gender and Imperialism* (forthcoming, 1993).
3 Indeed, the degree to which the *Eeufees* papered over fatal divisions within the white populace, became most manifest in 1988, when during the height of the State of Emergency, no less than two competing Treks set out to re-enact

the re-enactment, each sponsored by two bitterly rivalrous white nationalist parties.

4 As Ginwala notes: 'A pattern had been established of grassroots mobilization and participation by women, while dealing with the authorities at the local or national level was to remain the province of men.' 90:

5 Constitution, 1919.

6 As Gaitskell and Unterhalter (1989) have argued, the ideology of the 'Mother of the Nation' differs in some important respects from the iconography of the *volksmoeder* in Afrikaner nationalism.

7 On 9 August 1985, the 29th anniversary of South African Women's Day, the ANC's Women's Section called on women to 'take up arms against the enemy. In the past we have used rudimentary homemade weapons like petrol bombs. Now is the time that we use modern weapons.'

8 The ANC delegation to the Nairobi Conference on Women in 1985 declared: 'It would be suicidal for us to adopt feminist ideas. Our enemy is the system and we cannot exhaust our energies on women's issues.'

9 At a seminar entitled 'Feminism and National Liberation', convened by the Women's Section of the ANC in London in 1989, a representative from SAYCO (South African Youth Congress) exclaimed: 'How good it feels that feminism is finally accepted as a legitimate school of thought in our struggles and is not seen as a foreign ideology.'

References

ANDERSON, B. (1983, 1991) *Imagined Communities* London: Verso.

BALIBAR, E. and WALLERSTEIN, I (1991) *Race, Nation, Class: Ambiguous Identities* London: Verso.

BHABHA, H. K. (1991) *Nation and Narration* London: Routledge.

BOEHMER, E. (1991) 'Stories of women and mothers: gender and nationalism in the early fiction of Flora Nwapa' in NASTA (1991).

BRINK, E. (1990) 'Man-made women: gender, class and the ideology of the Volksmoeder' in Walker, C. (1990) editor, *Women and Gender in Southern Africa to 1945* London: James Currey.

BUCK-MORSS, Susan (1989) *The Dialectics of Seeing. Walter Benjamin and the Arcades Project* Cambridge, Mass.: MIT Press.

DAVIDOFF, L and HALL, C (1987) *Family Fortunes. Men and Women of the English Middle Class 1780–1850* London: Hutchinson.

ENLOE, C. (1989) *Bananas, Beaches and Bases. Making Feminist Sense of International Politics* Berkeley: University of California Press.

FABIAN, J (1983) *Time and the Other. How Anthropology Makes its Object* New York: Columbia University Press.

FANON, F. (1963) *The Wretched of the Earth* London: Penguin.

—— (1965) *A Dying Colonialism* New York: Monthly Review Press.

GAITSKELL, D. and UNTERHALTER, E (1989) 'Mothers of the nation: a comparative analysis of nation, race and motherhood in Afrikaner nationalism and the African National Congress' in YUVAL-DAVIS and ANTHIAS (1989).

GELLNER, E. (1964) *Thought and Change* London: Weidenfeld & Nicolson.

GINWALA, F. (1990) 'Women and the African National Congress 1912–1943', *Agenda*, 8, 1990, 77–93.

HOBSBAWM, E. (1990) *Nations and Nationalism Since 1780* Cambridge: Cambridge University Press.

HOFMEYR, Isabel (1987) 'Building a Nation from Words: Afrikaans Language, Literature and Ethnic Identity, 1902–1924' in **MARKS, S** and **TRAPIDO, S**.

JAYAWARDENA, K (1986) *Feminism and Nationalism in the Third World* London: Zed Press.

KANDIYOTI, D. (1991) 'Identity and its Discontents: Women and the Nation' **MILLENIUM**: *Journal of International Studies* 20, 3, 429–43.

LODGE, T. (1991) 'Charters from the Past: The African National Congress and its Historiographical Traditions' in *Radical History Review* 46/7, 161–89.

MARKS, S. and **TRAPIDO, S** (1987) editors *The Politics of Race, Class and Nationalism in Twentieth Century South Africa* London: Longmans.

MOHANTY, C (1991) 'Under Western Eyes: Feminist Scholarship and Colonial Discourses' in **MOHANTY, C., RUSSO, A,** and **TORRES, L** editors (1991) *Third World Women and the Politics of Feminism* Indiana: Bloomington.

MOODIE, T. D. (1975) *The Rise of Afrikanerdom. Power, Apartheid, and the Afrikaner Civil Religion* Berkeley: University of California Press.

MPAMA, J. (1937) in *Umsebenzi* 26 June.

NAIRN, T. (1977) *The Break-up of Britain* London: New Left Books.

NASTA, S. (1991) editor, *Motherlands. Black Women's Writing from Africa, the Caribbean and South Asia* London: The Women's Press.

O' MEARA, D (1983) *Volkskapitalisme. Class, Capital and Ideology in the Development of Afrikaner Nationalism 1934–1948* Cambridge: Cambridge University Press.

RENAN, E. (1990) 'What is a nation?' in **BHABHA, H. K.**

YUVAL-DAVIS, N. and **ANTHIAS, F.** (1989) editors, *Women-Nation-State* London: Macmillan.

WOMEN AS ACTIVISTS; WOMEN AS SYMBOLS: A Study of the Indian Nationalist Movement

Suruchi Thapar

Introduction

India's struggle for independence is of tremendous importance in the history of anti-colonial movements. The nationalist movement set the precedent of achieving independence through non-violence and thus a whole new philosophy based on *ahimsa*[1] was born. The culmination of the movement in the partition on religious grounds of a country as big and culturally diverse as India was also significant. However, arguably the most important aspect of this movement for Independence from a historical point of view was that it saw mass participation by Indian women, women who had till then been confined to the domestic sphere.

The contribution of women to the Independence movement was significant. They were involved in diverse nationalist activities, both within and outside the home. Within the home they spun and wove *khadi*, held classes to educate other women and contributed significantly to nationalist literature in the form of articles, poems and propaganda material. Shelter and nursing care were also provided to nationalist leaders who were in hiding from the British authorities. Outside the home *Prabhat feris* were organized in which women from all castes and classes would walk to the local temple singing songs to rouse the nationalist and patriotic feelings of the people. In addition they held meetings and demonstrations, took part in *satyagraha*, picketed toddy and foreign-cloth shops, went to prison and also suffered brutalities at the hands of the British police. Lastly, when the nationalist leadership were in gaol, the women took over the leadership roles and provided guidance to the movement.

In various writings on the nationalist movement it is argued that both the participation and leadership of women's activities was provided by 'middle-class women'. However, this article tries to show that middle-class women were not a homogeneous and undifferentiated category. Age and religion informed the consciousness of women as much as their class background, and also served to divide the class.

The nationalist project gained major benefits from the active participation of women as mentioned above. It also managed to make a significant impact on a susceptible populace by projecting women as powerful symbols of a 'unified' nation. To this end the concepts of 'motherhood' and 'femininity' were modified in accordance with the prevailing political ideology. In what follows, therefore, I first examine the formulation of various constructs of women and their use to the leaders of the nationalist project for the furtherance of their political aims. I also attempt to show how these constructs were modified, together with the attributes of 'femininity' and 'motherhood', to suit the changing requirements of the nationalist movement and its leaders.

The construction of the 'new' woman

In the late nineteenth century the construction of the 'new woman' was an issue central to nationalist discourse. This was also the time when the status of women in Indian society became a political issue and focus of debate and controversy. The position and status of women was, in British eyes, an indicator of the 'modernization' of a country. It also reflected on the ability of its citizens to rule themselves. Institutions of sati, polygamy, female infanticide, purdah and child-marriage came under British criticism.

Amongst Indian reformers, Hindu culture by contrast was regarded as superior to Western models. At the same time, it was recognized that, in order to avoid British criticism, Hindu culture had to be rendered more consistent with Western ideas of liberalism and humanitarianism. (Agnew, 1979: 4) These Western values were seen to form a part of the 'material' domain, a domain dominated by Western science, technology and methods of statecraft. Opposed to this domain was the 'spiritual' domain, which was seen as representative of the 'true identity' of the Indian people. (Chatterjee, 1989: 23) The woman was supposed to be the guardian of the 'spiritual' domain. The task before the nationalist leaders was now to protect the inherent qualities of the 'spiritual domain'. This was because while in the material domain colonizers had 'subjugated' the colonized, that is the non-European people, it was in the spiritual domain that no encroachments had taken place. Thus there was a perceived need to protect the sanctity of this domain, a domain representing the culture and 'Indianness' of the people.

However, the nationalist leaders also realized that the 'spiritual' domain had to be made more consistent with the outside world and its new ideas of equality and liberalism. Thus the construct of the 'new woman' was formulated. This construct was relevant to women from the middle class, the demographic section which was the cornerstone of the nation in late colonial India. The success of this construct was dependent on the formal education of women. Education was viewed as a means to enhance the social presence of Indian women and enable them to adapt to a changing external situation. Education was also seen as making the 'new woman' more responsible towards her familial duties. She was supposed to be inculcated, through education, with the virtues of cleanliness, companionship, discipline and self-control (Borthwick, 1984: 358). These qualities were added to her traditional role in the family, without changing the basic social relationship characterized by male dominance.

The spiritual role of the new woman was not only represented as a mark of the superiority of Hindu as compared to 'alien' culture, but also a sign of women's 'newly acquired freedom'. (Chatterjee, 1989: 245). However, in order that the new woman's 'newly acquired freedom' still be contained within the parameters set by the nationalist leaders, the 'common woman' construct was created. The 'common woman', as opposed to the 'new woman', was coarse, promiscuous and vulgar. The common women were the nautch girls, street-vendors, fisherwomen, 'washer women', to cite but a few. Besides lacking the veneer of gentility, these women, due to economic compulsion, were forced to eke out an existence on the streets. They thus lacked the attributes of docility and submissiveness which were ingrained in middle-class women.

The creation of the 'common woman' construct set moral limits on women's behaviour and their code of conduct. The choice for a woman was thus limited to being either a 'new woman' or a 'common woman' – a choice imposed by nationalist leaders. It can be argued that there were benefits to be gained by the nationalist movement and its leaders in the creation of these constructs. I would suggest that these came from the way the 'new woman' construct could explain and contain the activities of women (including ensuring that they adhered to non-violent activities during their participation in the Independence movement). The construction of the 'common woman', on the other hand, eliminated any possibility of a public exploration of the differences and conflicts that women, in the course of their political participation, could experience.

Closely associated with the construct of the 'new woman' were the concepts of 'femininity' and 'motherhood'. Femininity had to be projected in a particular way so that while it facilitated the Indian man's efforts to prove his 'masculinity' in the external domain, it also maintained traditional patriarchal relations within the family by offering no threat to the dominance of male attitudes. Lack of 'masculinity' was a pertinent issue around which India's unfitness for self-rule and the need for British rule were justified by the colonial officials. English 'manly reserve' and 'self-control' were generally portrayed as attributes of 'civilized men'. *Mother India*, the controversial book by Katherine Mayo, which highlighted 'inertia, helplessness, lack of initiative and originality, sterility of enthusiasm' (Mayo, 1917: 24) as some of the characteristics of Indian men, was thus one of the many which questioned the adequacy of Indian 'masculinity'.

It has also been noted by Mrinalini Sinha how on many occasions
the colonial rulers attempted to express disdain for Indian 'masculinity',
especially that of Bengali men. The Indian Consent Act 1891, a colonial
move towards prohibiting consummation of marriage by Indian men
before their wives became twelve years of age, was provided as proof of
the 'depraved nature of Indian gender relations' (Sinha, 1987: 224). It
was argued by the legislators that consummation before a designated
age was a feature associated with 'effeminate' men (Sinha, 1987: 226)
who lacked the masculine qualities of self-restraint and self-control.

In this context, it was essential for the nationalist leaders to project
'femininity' in ways which would enhance the 'masculine' or worldly
virtues of Indian men. The concept of 'femininity' in the 'new woman'
construct which thus emerged was based on mythology, literature and
history. The mythical figures of Sita and Savitri were considered the
epitome of ideal Indian womanhood. The woman was supposed to be
devoted to her husband and to show reverence for elders. In addition she
was supposed to be her husband's *Ardhangini* (complementary half)
and *Sahadharmini* (helpmate), as well as to possess the virtues of
benevolence and self-sacrifice. There was at the same time equal stress
on her acquiring the practical skills of running a house and rearing
children. All these virtues were considered non-threatening in the
traditional male hierarchy.

The concept of 'motherhood', like that of 'masculinity', was also
subject to British criticism. This was because early motherhood, a result
of child marriages, was seen by the British as one of the causes of the
depraved nature of the Indian men. With reference to early 'motherhood', Mayo commented,

> Force motherhood upon her at the earliest possible moment. Rear her
> weakling son in intensive vicious practices that drain his small vitality
> day by day. Give him no outlet in sports. Give him habits that make him,
> by the time he is thirty years of age, a decrepit and querulous old wreck –
> and will you ask what has sapped the energy of his manhood (Mayo,
> 1917: 25)

In the Indian tradition the mother has always been deified. Thus,
for example, goddesses like Durga, Saraswati, Sita and Vaishno were
regularly represented as mothers.[2] This sanctified image of the mother
was now considered an important vehicle by the nationalist leaders to
convey the idea of a strong 'civilization' to the British. It was argued that
the west did not stress *mattabhav* (motherhood) qualities as they were
in India (Lakhanpal, 1934: 70). 'Motherhood', as thus defined, implied a
woman not only loving or caring for her children, but also producing
healthy progeny (the mother as race nourisher). She had also to
undertake the task of educating her progeny to be the future enlightened citizens of India.

> In the extremes of honour and serfdom accorded to womanhood Asia is
> one. It has messages concerning the sanctity of life, the vocation of woman

'*Gandhi The Protector of India*'

as race nourisher. . . . None holds this Oriental culture more tenaciously, more authentically, than its women (Cousins, 1930: 12).

The 'new woman' in the twentieth century

By the early years of the twentieth century, the construct of the 'new woman' and the associated ideas of 'femininity' and 'motherhood' were beginning to be modified to meet the requirements of a changing political atmosphere. Indian society was already undergoing changes in matters related to gender, and the political movement for Independence was gaining momentum. The emergence of Gandhi on the political scene in the 1920s as the nationalist leader had tremendous impact on women. His ideas about women's roles in the nationalist movement were considered 'revolutionary' for that period. Though he believed in gender-specific roles, he was very critical of those roles that cloistered women in ignorance and affected them adversely, like *purdah*, dowry and the devadasi (temple dancers) tradition.

It is pertinent to discuss how Gandhi envisaged the participation of women in nationalist politics. He realized the significant role women could play in the nationalist movement by their active participation. Also, he realized how the construct of the 'new woman' had to be modified to bring women out of their homes. He argued that the qualities of self-sacrifice and 'silent suffering' were ingrained in Indian women. Thus women were ideally suited to participate in his movement, the core concepts of which are *ahimsa* (non-violence in thought, action and deed) and *satyagraha*: 'If non-violence is the law of our being, the future is with women' (*Young India*, 15.12.21).

Gandhi thus stressed those attributes of women which were beneficial for his political campaign. An integral feature of Gandhi's civil disobedience movement, and one for which women were particularly suited, was spinning and weaving *khadi*. Gandhi advocated self-reliance by weaving one's own cloth and boycotting foreign cloth. It was easy to identify spinning and weaving *khadi* as women's *dharma* (the eternal law of the Hindu cosmos) or duty, since it was primarily women's responsibility to feed and clothe her family. Sarladevi Sarabhai, an activist, acknowledged her motivation to join the nationalist movement 'as a desire to fulfil her *dharma*' (Agnew, 1979: 56). Spinning on the *charkha* (spinning wheel) was an integral part of Gandhi's Constructive Programme and his campaign against the colonial masters. The *charkha* was identified as the national symbol and later incorporated in the national flag of India. Spinning and weaving *khadi* enhanced the significance of women's contribution to the movement in their own eyes. Also, the more tradition-bound women could have the satisfaction of participating without going on the streets.

In the 1930s, however, Gandhi began to encourage the emergence of women into public space, and the sanctity of the home that he had earlier stressed was disturbed. At this point, he realized the dilemma of distinguishing 'women of the street' from 'women on the street', because paradoxically the 'new woman' had to picket 'on the streets' herself. One of the worries of the women activists involved in street demonstrations was about distinguishing themselves from 'women of the street'. An example of this can be seen during the civil disobedience movement in the 1930s when prostitutes from Kanpur, Uttar Pradesh (who fell under the category of the 'common woman') were stopped from joining the movement and were said to be 'unfit to sit near other ladies' by members of the District Congress Committee (*The Leader*, 14.5.30: 6). The nationalist leader Gandhi himself refused to accept the prostitutes as Congress members unless they gave up their 'unworthy profession'.

Thus the 'new woman' construct had to be modified to allow for women taking to the streets. The modified construct incorporated qualities like strength of will, steadfastness of purpose and fortitude in the face of adversity. The woman of this construct was supposed to bear stoically long separations from her husband and patiently bear the mental and physical trauma of his imprisonments, his maltreatment at the hands of British police and his disappearance for days on end. Yet when the need arose, this woman was exhorted to come out of the home and undertake leadership roles in the absence of her husband (Nehru, 1949: 214).

Despite all the above, Gandhi remained a 'traditionalist' in the domestic sphere. His construct called for no reorganization of familial duties. In fact, he believed that political participation could not take place at the cost of domestic duties.

> It became my conviction that procreation and consequent care of children were inconsistent with public service. . . . If I wanted to devote myself to the service of the community . . . I must relinquish the desire for children and wealth and live the life of a *vanaprastha* (Gandhi, 1942: 196).

Gandhi's stress on the familial responsibilities of women may be explained by his need to secure support from the 'guardians' of women by assuring men of the safety and protection of their women. As Geraldine Forbes points out, 'had Gandhi not also paid attention to the attitudes of the guardian, it is unlikely he would have been successful' (Forbes, 1988: 67) Thus, while Gandhi encouraged women's political participation, he was careful that their activities did not threaten men's masculinity in any way.

'Masculinity' in the 1930s was still as sensitive an issue as it was in the nineteenth century. A simple example of how nationalist leaders were conscious of this issue can be seen in the reason Gandhi gave for excluding women from the first salt *satyagraha* on 6 April 1930.

> Just as Hindus do not harm a cow, the British do not attack women as far as possible. For Hindus it would be cowardice to take a cow to the battlefield. In the same way it would be cowardice for us to have women accompany us (Gandhi, 1971: 12).

The associated concept of 'motherhood' was also broadened in the twentieth century to incorporate more qualities. The image of the 'nurturer of civilization' of Indian mothers was expanded to include the idea of the mother as 'defender of civilization'.[3] The nationalist leaders realized the significance of the concept of a unified 'motherland', a motherland that stretched from the 'Himalayas to the Indian Ocean'. The mother of the nineteenth century was now identified with the 'motherland' or *Bharat mata*. Literally translated *Bharat mata* means 'mother India'. This idea aligned the duties and responsibilities of the mother with the duties of a woman towards her nation. *Bharat mata* was projected as the ultimate mother, with all Indians as her sons and daughters. This mother, when in danger, could summon her 'countless' children to her aid.

The idea of *Bharat mata* served a dual purpose. Firstly, the allegiance of women as mothers to their nation prevented women from expressing displeasure when their sons/fathers/brothers were hauled in to gaols or thrown in *kala pani*. Secondly, the deified image of a 'single' mother of the whole nation, whose honour had to be protected, aroused the national sentiments of the population as a whole.

The idea of *Bharat mata* was propagated through poetry, literature and the movies. Invariably, the image was of a crowned and beautiful woman in 'shackles' weeping 'tears of blood', or of the same woman holding aloft a trident and leading her countless sons and daughters to battle. Poets like Bal Krishna Sharma Navin (1898–1960), Harbans Rai Bachhan (1907–) and Mahadevi Verma (1907–87) propagated the concept of *Bharat Mata*. One poem by Bal Krishna Sharma, 'The Song of the Morning Breeze' highlights, for example, the idea of a mother in distress.

> May the nectar like milk of the mother turn into bitter gall.
> May the tears of her eyes dry up to leave a stream of blood behind.
> Hey poet, string together the words that will be cataclysmic (Sharma, 1989: 20).

Such symbolic representations of women enabled them to emerge as active participants in national processes. But it is pertinent to note that the nationalist leaders benefited the most from the manipulations of representations of women. The benefits to women of participation in the nationalist movement, by contrast, were always limited by their responsibilities for 'women's work' in the home.

Nationalist activities of women

The mass participation of women in the nationalist movement is a well-recognized historical reality. Their activities within the movement were, however, diverse. While some women participated actively on the streets, others just gave support to the movement. One activity which received a particularly eager response from women was, for example, the breaking of salt laws. Salt was a commodity that affected women from all walks of life equally. Women all over the country marched to the sea depots to manufacture salt, an activity which was illegal.

Women were also made responsible by Gandhi for picketing liquor and foreign cloth shops. The women would sit outside the shops and dissuade customers from making purchases. If this tactic did not work they would lie in front of the stores and effectively stop customers from going in. Often picketing relied on the social pressure that it could exert – so for example most of the women involved in pickets were from the same caste as the men visiting the liquor stores.

Other forms of agitation involved leading processions, holding meetings and courting arrest. Often, after leading a procession, women leaders would make speeches exhorting their fellow-activists to achieve greater heights of patriotism. In some meetings proscribed literature was also read. Many women were thrown behind bars: so, for example, of the 80,000 people arrested during the salt *satyagraha*, 17,000 were women (Jayawardena, 1986: 10).

Women who did not take an active part contributed by spreading the message of *Swadeshi*. They also held classes in various *ashrams* on spinning and weaving *khadi*. The most visible participation in all these activities came from 'middle class' women. There is, moreover, a presupposition in most historical tracts on Indian nationalism that middle-class women were united on the basis of their gender, shared a common political goal, i.e., the anti-colonial struggle, and had the same political consciousness. It can, however, be argued that middle-class women were not an homogeneous and undifferentiated category. The political motivations and activities of women differed on the basis of age, religion and political consciousness.

The projection of a unified political role is often argued on the basis of the number of women participants, in such formulations as, 'in an audience of five thousand, no less than two thousand were women' or 'thousands of women strode down to the sea like proud warriors' (Baig, 1958: 19). Yet what this obscures are all the conflicts and differences of opinion on participation that existed in the nationalist movement. Not all women shared the same political opinions towards their activities and organizational tasks. Aparna Basu has mentioned the women of the Nehru family having responded to Gandhi's call:

> Not only Vijaylakshmi Pandit and Krishna but the aged Swarup Rani and the ailing Kamala were in the frontline of leadership . . . organising processions, addressing meetings and picketing foreign cloth (Basu, 1976: 27).

However, the reality was more complex. Not all women took to political participation like 'proud warriors' or because of their awakened consciousness of modern Indian womanhood. There were conflicts with women's lives which were raised in the course of their participation.

Vijaylakshmi Pandit, in her autobiography, mentions that her mother, Swarup Rani, found it difficult to adjust to the changed lifestyle and the constant infringement of her privacy which activism produced:

> This was a time of great domestic strain and constant adjustments were asked for. Mother felt acutely miserable over all that was happening. How could she take sides (with husband or son) or understand this new 'Mahatma' whose business, if anything, should have been to look after people's morals instead of meddling in family matters (Pandit, 1979: 89).

Thus even as women stood ready to respond to Gandhi's call, they were beset by guilt and anguish at having to neglect their homes and children. They were thus torn in two directions – one towards their duty towards the nation and one towards the family.

The activities of women from the middle class differed also according to age. The activities of the younger generation were markedly different from the activities of women following the Gandhian non-violent programme. The leaders of the first nationalist generation were quick to identify the potential in the younger generation. When Pandit Nehru and Subhas Bose, constituting the radical wing of the Congress, founded the Independence League in 1928, Jawaharlal Nehru commented:

> After long suppression the spirit of youth is up in arms against all forms of authoritarianism, and is seeking an outlet in many ways and directions. Youth leagues have sprung up in all parts of the country and individual young men and women, weary of the continual and barren strife of many of their elders, are groping for a path which might lead them to a fuller realisation of themselves (*The Leader*, 24.3.28: 7).

As one activist, Vinodini Sinha, commented, 'Women of the older generation lacked the courage to try and establish new social norms which had been kindled' (Rao, 1989–90: 256). Young middle-class women, by contrast, were active in organizing underground activities. Revolutionary organizations increased their sabotage activities in the 1930s. The province of Bengal was very active. Santi and Suniti, young girls in their teens, shot dead Stevens, District Magistrate of Comilla in December 1931 (Basu, 1976: 32). In Delhi, Roop Vati Jain, aged seventeen, was in charge of a bomb factory under Chandra Shekhar Azad. This factory produced picric acid, nitro-glycerine, gun-cotton and other ingredients for bombs.

Most of these women had earlier served as members of the youth league, organized by the Congress. In the Benares bomb case, Miss Mrinalini and Radharani Debi had been members of the Benares Youth League and had earlier taken part in picketing. However, disenchantment with the non-violent programme caused them to resort to terrorism, until they were arrested under Sections 4 and 5 of the Explosive Substances Act and 19F Arms Act (*Hindustan Times*, 22.4.31: 5; *Amrit Bazar Patrika (ABP)*, 5.5.31: 10).

Just as men and women were positioned differently within the same class, women were positioned differently with respect to each other within the middle class. Thus, for example, the religious imagery used by young terrorist women was different from that used by women of the non-violent programme. Women involved in sabotage stressed the destructive, aggressive and violent qualities of the feminine deities (Shakti and Kali). Differences in perception due to religion also affected the motivations and nature of women's activities. Though Muslim women participated in the nationalist movement, they did not do so in such large numbers as Hindus. Women like Bi Amman, Begum Mohammed Ali, Begum Hasrat Mohani and Mrs Abdul Kadir did, however, contribute actively to the movement, especially by picketing shops owned by Muslims who resented the activities of Hindu women. Muslim women's participation also introduced the important issue of *purdah* to the nationalist movement. *Purdah* was an issue for social reform brought up in women's meetings and conferences. In a nationalist song composed in honour of Urmilla Devi (an activist in Meerut), it was stated, 'Hey womankind, leave your comfortable homes, give your bangles to the menfolk, leave your veils behind, come out in the streets and bazaars (Gupta, 1931: 11). Giving 'bangles' to men as well as leaving the 'veil' behind reflects the drive towards sexual reform often voiced in nationalist songs and poems. Yet it should be noted that Gandhi's movement, which encouraged women to come out of their seclusion, attracted more Hindu women than Muslim. Muslim women from the middle class did not in general discard *purdah*, and their participation in processions was more a gesture of solidarity than a challenge to the *purdah* tradition (*The Leader*, 9 July 1930: 13).

A possible reason for Muslim women retaining the *burqa* was the resentment expressed by their menfolk towards women's activities outside the home. Some Muslim men, in anonymous letters to newspapers, commented that even though Hindu men did not protest at the use of their women in picketing liquor and cloth shops, it was affecting their Muslim women who, 'brought up within the *purdah* tradition', must suffer when suddenly called upon to interfere with strangers in the bazaars and made to 'sit publicly' with male shopkeepers. They considered the activities that their women had been involved in as 'unwomanly' and 'immodest' acts (White, 1930: 10).

Seen in the light of the construction of the 'new woman', the difference between Muslim and Hindu opinions is particularly significant. For the Muslims, whose womenfolk were said to perceive men other than their fathers and brothers as threats to their morals and chastity, activities which were regarded as 'respectable' by Hindu nationalist leaders were seen as 'immodest'. Clearly, then, the construction of 'new woman' was hardly a homogeneous category, either in terms of class, generation or religion.

Kali, 1908

Conclusion

Though the history of the nationalist movement has been rewritten on many occasions, existing histories share a common lacuna on the plane of gender. This article, while drawing links between gender and nationalism, and between gender and colonialism, has discussed the 'experience' of women in the nationalist movement in India. I do not intend to provide an authentic 'voice' for Indian women, but I have tried to expose the contradictions that arise in analyses focusing on issues of gender, nationalism and colonialism.

In existing discussions of nationalist discourse, two different levels of analysis have been prevalent. Firstly, there has been an attempt by the nationalist movement and its leaders to project a 'correct' picture of the nationalist activities of middle-class women. One of the consequences of providing a 'correct picture' has been that women have been projected as a homogeneous and uniform category. Consequently, women have been misrepresented in historical tracts and the diversity of their activity, varying political consciousness and the conflicts and ambiguities to which they were prey have been downplayed. Women harboured different attitudes and opinions on the basis of their consciousness, age and religion. This article has also tried to show that the nationalist movement benefited both by projecting women as a homogeneous category and constructing them as special role models.

On the second level, Indian historians have reproduced this 'correct' picture of the nationalist movement. Though it is difficult to identify *why* Indian historians have reproduced nationalist discourse and what benefits they gained by so doing, it remains clear that, at both levels, women's activities have been marginalized.

Though this article has not taken up the academic debate on misrepresentation of women in historical records, it has tried to show that the success of some political movements is dependent on women's contribution. The Indian nationalist movement benefited not only from the nationalist activities of women but also from the way it confined its women to various constructs and role-models.

Glossary

ahimsa   The doctrine of non-violence

ashram   This literally means a place of rest for the hermit and the wandering ascetic, but in modern India it means a dwelling-place offering a life of peace and solitude.

burqa   A one-piece covering worn by Muslim women in public places. Apart from the mesh through which one can see, the *burqa* covers the wearer from head to toe

charkha   A wooden spinning wheel operated by hand on which *khadi* cloth was spun. *Charkha* was the basis of the *handloom* industry, as opposed to the *power loom* industries encouraged by the British.

civil disobedience	Withdrawal of all voluntary association with the British Government and its institutions. Civil disobedience also incorporated non-payment of taxes
dharma	This can be variously interpreted as a doctrine of righteousness, sacred law, or a general code of conduct which is appropriate to each class and each stage in the life of an individual.
kala pani	This term implied lifelong incarceration in the most brutal conditions, often leading to death. The most common cause of death was 'black-water' (*kali-pani*) fever.
Kali	Goddess of destruction
khadi	Coarse, hand-spun cloth. *Khadi* was also a cultural symbol of nationalism and *swaraj*. In Delhi a *Khadi* Pracharak Mandal, an association for the promotion of *khadi*, started a monthly magazine of its own called *Khadi Sandesh* (Message of *Khadi*). It was published in English and Hindi (*Hindustan Times*, 7 January 1931: 6).
nautch girls	Dancing girls mainly of low caste. May or may not be prostitutes
prabhat pheris	Literally translated it means 'morning around'. It comprised groups of women and men going around various localities singing nationalist and devotional songs.
purdah	Originally derived from a Persian word meaning 'curtain', it carries an implicit meaning of subordination. For example, in Hinduism women are encouraged to remain inside the home or to cover their heads when in public view. *Purdah* is also the veil often used by women of the Muslim communities which leaves only the eyes showing, the rest of the body being completely covered.
satyagraha	Social boycott of the legal and political institutions of the British Government
Shakti	Goddess of strength and vitality
Sita *and* Savitri	Two women figures from Hindu mythology. They are noted for their obedience and devotion to their husbands
swadeshi	Literally translated this means 'for my country'. The concept was promoted to encourage the Indians to spin and weave indigenous cloth and forsake foreign cloth. *Swadeshi* also incorporated all activities that promoted self-reliance.
swaraj	Independence
vanaprastha	leaving home and family for the forest to become a hermit, often referred to as the third stage of life.

Notes

Suruchi Thapar is a second-year Ph.D. student in the Department of Interdisciplinary Women's Studies, University of Warwick. She is working on feminism and nationalism from 1925–42 in Uttar Pradesh (a state of India).

I am grateful to Joanna Liddle, Carol Walkowitz and Terry Lovell for their comments on earlier drafts of the paper. An earlier version of this paper was presented at the 'Gender and Colonialism' Conference, Galway, Ireland in May 1992.

1 See Glossary for terms not defined in the text.
2 A poem entitled 'The Jingle of the Shackles' written by Jagannatha Prasada Arora stresses a similar point. 'Mother of India, may you be praised, may you be praised, may your progeny be brave and bold, may their victory emerge like the Sun, may they be fearless like Bhishma and Arjuna [mythological figures].' (Arora, 1930)
3 Deborah Gaitskell and Elaine Unterhalter, with reference to South Africa, have pointed out how different representations of 'Afrikaaner motherhood' were tied up with the concepts of race and nation. For example, imperial control over Boer republics was referred to as the 'suffering of Afrikaaner mothers', or in 1914, during the formation of the first Afrikaaner National Party, there was stress on women's role as mother (Gaitskell and Unterhalter, 1989).

References

AGNEW, Vijay (1979) *Elite Women in Indian Politics* Delhi: Vikas Publications.

ARORA, Jagnath (1930) *Beriyon Ki Jhankar* Benares: PP Hin.B.298.

BAIG, Tara Ali (1958) *Women of India* Delhi: Ministry of Information and Broadcasting.

BASU, Aparna (1976) 'The role of women in the Indian struggle for freedom' in NANDA (1976).

BORTHWICK, Meredith (1984) *The Changing Role of Women in Bengal 1849–1905* New Jersey: Princeton University Press.

CHATTERJEE, Partha (1989) 'The Nationalist resolution of the women's question' in SANGHARI and VAID (1989).

COUSINS, Margaret (1930) 'Women and Oriental Culture' *The Leader* 9 January.

FORBES, Geraldine (1988) 'The politics of respectability: Indian women and the Indian National Congress' in LOW (1988).

GAITSKELL, Deborah and UNTERHALTER, Elaine (1989) 'Mothers of the nation: A comparative analysis of nation, race and motherhood in Afrikaaner nationalism and the African National Congress' in YUVAL-DAVIS and ANTHIAS (1989).

GANDHI, Mahatma (1971) *The Collected Works of Mahatma Gandhi* vol xliii Ahmedabad: Navajivan.

GANDHI, Mohandas (1942) *Women and Social Injustice* Ahmedabad: Navajivan Publishing House.

GUPTA, Gautam (1931) *Inquilab Ki Lahar* PIB.67/19 Bukselar: India Office Library.

JAYAWARDENA, Kumari (1986) *Feminism and Nationalism in the Third World* London: Zed Press.

KIMMEL, M. (1987) *Changing Men: New Directions in Research on Men and Masculinity* New Dehli: Sage Publications.

LAKHANPAL, Chandravati (1934) *Striyon Ki Stiti* Gurukul: India Office Library.

LOW, David (1988) editor, *The Indian National Congress: Centenary Hindsights*, Delhi: Oxford University Press.

MAYO, Katherine (1917) *Mother India* London: Howard Baker.

NANDA, Bisheswar (1976) *Indian Women: From Purdah to Modernity* Delhi: Vikas Publications.

NEHRU, Jawaharlal (1949) *An Autobiography* London: Bodley Head.

PANDIT, V. (1979) The Scope of happiness: a personal memoir. London: Nicholson.

RAO, Uma (1989–90) 'A generation apart: women in the national movement' *Samya Shakti* Vols. IV & V: 254–64.

RAO, Uma and DEVI, Meera (1984) 'Glimpses: UP women's responses to Gandhi, 1921–1930' *Samya Shakti* Vol. I, No. II: 21–32.

SANGHARI, Kum Kum and VAID, Sudesh (1989) editors, *Recasting Women: Essays in Colonial History* New Delhi: Kali for Women.

SATYAVATI, Kumari (1932) *Stree Darshan* Bihar: Gurukul Harpurjan.

SHARMA, Balkrisha (1989) *Mandakini* Delhi: NCERT.

SINHA, Mrinalini (1987) 'Colonial policy and the ideology of moral imperialism in late nineteenth century Bengal' in KIMMEL (1987).

WHITE, Leslie (1930) *The Leader*. 9 August.

YUVAL-DAVIS, Nira and ANTHIAS, Floya (1989) editors, *Women-Nation-State* London: Macmillan Press.

GENDER, NATIONALISMS AND NATIONAL IDENTITIES: Bellagio Symposium, July 1992

Catherine Hall

This year it must be clear to all of us that nationalism, far from being dead, is one of the most powerful forces in contemporary political life. The daily news, from the horrific events in the area which was once Yugoslavia, to the national and ethnic conflicts which threaten to break up the CIS, to the new cries for 'Germany for the Germans', all remind us that the death of state socialisms and the remapping of Europe has provided the opportunity for the rebirth of new nationalisms. At a more local and less serious level the British political parties find themselves unable to deal with the deep splits in their own ranks on the question of British 'national sovereignty' and Britain's relation to Europe. Being for or against Europe does not neatly coincide with allegiance to one or other of the major parties and issues about national identity are daily sharply debated in the press, on radio and on television. Indeed, 'national identity' and what is meant by that has become a hot topic. How national identity might relate to gender, however, is a less central subject.

Benedict Anderson's influential book *Imagined Communities. Reflections on the Origin and Spread of Nationalism*, first published in 1983, has done much to set the terms of debate on nations and nationalisms for the left. His critique of the failure of Marxism to deal with 'the national question', his notion of the nation as an 'imagined community', imagined both politically and culturally, his insistence on the historical specificity of meanings of nation and nationalism, his emphasis on the place of print-culture in the construction of the nation and his suggestive comment that it might be helpful to think of nationalism as akin to religion, have all fuelled discussion and further research. But Anderson is not interested in questions of gender and sexuality and feminists who comb his book for inspiration on ways of thinking about the particular relation of women or men to the nation, or nationalism to feminism, will find little joy.

In July 1992, a symposium was held at Bellagio in Italy which brought together a few of those who are now trying to think about those connexions.[1] Its title was 'Gender, Nationalisms and National Identities' and over three days of discussion we tried to think collectively about gender and nation. The symposium was funded by the Rockefeller Foundation, which owns a spectacularly beautiful villa on Lake Como which is available for such events. In addition the Nuffield Foundation gave funds for administrative support. It was organized by the journal *Gender and History*, with the support of the Women's Studies Programme at the Johns Hopkins University. Twenty-four people attended, twenty-one women and three men, from Australia, Italy, France, Norway, the US and the UK. All, except the organizing group from *Gender and History*, were invited because of the current research they are doing and its relation to the topics under discussion.

Since we were committed to a comparative approach we invited historians (the majority group), anthropologists, specialists in development studies and cultural theorists and critics. Papers were commissioned for the symposium and were pre-circulated so that the emphasis throughout could be on debate. We were well aware as to how

The View Over Lake Como

selective we were necessarily being in the topics which we covered. (The fact that the Rockefeller Foundation do not provide travel funds severely limited possible participants as everyone had to find their own travel funds.)

Seven sessions were held, each of two and a half hours, and sessions were organized both chronologically and thematically. We opened with the emergence of new nations, new gendered identities and new histories associated with the American and French Revolutions. We then looked at debates over national identity in England in the nineteenth century, particularly in the context of a discussion about the connexions between ethnicity, race, gender and class. The third session was concerned with the complex relationship between nationalisms and feminisms in the late nineteenth and twentieth centuries in Norway, Sweden and Greece. We then considered the contrast between contemporary debates in Romania and Australia over questions of gender and national identity. Further sessions debated the construction of Indian, Iranian and Egyptian national identities in the nineteenth and twentieth centuries, the changing relation between nation and gender, and the place of colonialism and anti-colonial struggles in these specific histories.

From this rich brew it is hard to identify what became the most helpful and productive debates. My choice is obviously a personal one, linked to my own particular interests and work. The fact that we opened the symposium with a discussion of the American and French revolutions in part reflected the extent to which Anderson has set the terms of debate on nation and nationalisms, for he sees those revolutions as providing the models for new kinds of nations. Lata Mani, an Indian feminist working in the US, provocatively raised the question towards the end of the symposium as to what the effects would have been on our discussions if we had started with India, or with Egypt, or with Iran. Looking first at non-Western models of nation, or models which were framed by the colonial experience, would undoubtedly have shaped the debates differently and might have contributed to our stated intention of not centring on the metropolis as the fount of nation and nationalisms.

In reflecting on different revolutionary experiences, in America, in France, in Iran, part of our concern was with the ways in which political change means the construction of new national identities and new ways of conceptualizing national belonging. National identities are, of course, always in the process of constitution, never fixed and stable, though often drawing on a repertoire of traditions, myths and representations which are constantly reworked and rearticulated to different national projects. As Carroll Smith-Rosenberg, an American historian, argued, British and other European settlers in the thirteen colonies which made up pre-revolutionary 'America', had to find ways of making sense for themselves and others of their seizure of the land and the name of the 'new world' to which they had come. They had to learn to imagine themselves as not English or Scottish or Dutch but members of a new nation, forged through a colonial revolution. In the process, the white American man, the citizen, constituted his identity through the creation of boundaries between himself and those others also living in that land and having putative claims to forms of belonging to the new nation: the white American woman, the black man, the black woman, the red man, the red woman. National identities were thus distinctively gendered as well as being shaped by racial and ethnic differences. Exploring the historical conditions for the production of new national identities and the place of gender, race, ethnicity and class in that process provided one of our central themes over the three days.

The symbolic place of gender in the construction of national identities provided another. The gendering of nations and nationalisms provides many clues as to why, for example, women's active involvement in nationalist struggles does not result in their holding effective political power after independence. The common theme of the nation as female, which implies the gendering of the citizen as male, sets limits on the forms of national belonging available to women. Indeed, we often think of the state as masculine and discussions around this led us to try and clarify, not always terribly successfully, the distinction between nation and state. Women can often be conceptualized as 'mothers of the nation', an image which places their reproductive capacities as at the centre of their service to the nation. Familial language, ordering gender relations, is also frequently at the heart of the 'imagined community'. In the nationalist struggle in Egypt, for example, Beth Baron, an American historian, argued that the nation was imagined as a family whose sexual honour was to be redeemed from the humiliation of occupation. In Norway, Ida Blom, a Norwegian historian, suggested, the idea of the home became widened to the national home and this fed the early twentieth-century concept of the state as 'the people's home', which gave women direct access to state support but also enabled state definitions of gender-appropriate behaviour. In Soviet bloc countries, on the other hand, as Katherine Verderey, an American anthropologist, pointed out, the household became a very important site of opposition to the state. Meanwhile, as Joanna de Groot, a British historian of Iran reminded us, gender may be a central concern of nationalist movements yet women's interests may still be marginalized.

Closely related to this set of discussions was our exploration of the complex and contradictory relationship between nationalisms and feminisms. For nationalism has both made possible forms of activism for women which were previously impossible, and simultaneously limited their horizons. As Marilyn Lake, an Australian historian, suggested, the history of feminism in that country has been closely interwined with its relation to nationalism. Nationalism was a masculinist discourse, the marker of difference was the 'lone hand', the male bush worker. National identity was forged against the 'mother country' through the achievement of manly independence, against racial others, particularly the Chinese and Aboriginal peoples, and against the enslavements of domesticity.

For women, a stress on political citizenship in the nation-state was important and it was a matter of pride for early feminists that their enfranchisement coincided with the birth of the nation-state. If the nation needed population then maternalism could mean using the state to challenge the power of men and could be a vehicle for feminists. But maternalist policies might also be complicit with race and class oppressions, for Aboriginal women were ineligible for the rights associated with motherhood and citizenship and their children were taken from them, while working-class women were closely scrutinized, their 'failures' (to be middle class) scapegoated. Feminism, in other words, when aligned with nationalism, could deliver benefits for some women but not others.

Given that the majority of the participants of the symposium were historians, it was not surprising that another of the themes to which we returned was the place of historical narratives in the construction of national identities. Olwen Hufton, a British historian of France, opened up this debate with her analysis of the ways in which radical historians in nineteenth-century France explained the failure of the revolution of 1789, as they saw it, as due to women's conservatism and Catholicism. National histories have both marginalized women and demonized them. Ann Curthoys, an historian from Sydney, was able to give us a more optimistic account from contemporary Australia as to the difference which feminist historians have been able to make in the construction of new national histories. Australia, she argued, has been deeply preoccupied with the question of national identities in the last few years, a preoccupation fed by the bi-centennial, by women's politics and by the attempts by Aboriginal peoples to reclaim their heritage. In this conjuncture, feminist historians have been able to contribute to new versions of the national history, ones which place gender at the heart of the nation's project.

The relation between the Enlightenment concept of the nation, that nation forged in the revolutionary moment and committed to progress, and colonialism, was another question which we opened up. For what would nations be like if they were not part of the colonial dyad? In America, the destruction of one colonial relation (with Britain) and the construction of another (with native Americans and blacks) was central to the emergence of the independent nation. In nineteenth-century Britain, colonies were an essential prerequisite of the 'imagined community': in both these instances there would be no metropolis without the peripheries defining and sustaining it. In those countries which were colonized, the anti-colonial struggle was a necessary part of the nationalist movement and so nation was again defined against the colonial relation. In India one of the effects of this was that 'tradition', articulated in part through gender, as Samita Sen, an Indian historian living in Britain, pointed out in relation to the Bengali nationalist and reforming movement, was mobilized as a key component of the new nation in its definition of itself against the colonial power.

One of the most provocative questions raised, and certainly not answered, concerned the ways in which narratives of national identity become forms of individual subjectivity. What is the relation between the narratives which generate forms of identification with the nation and an individual's sense of self? Or, to put it another way, how is 'affect' mobilized on behalf of the nation? Furthermore, how might this relate to the erotic or the sexual – here the discussion drew on Katherine Verderey's material on the importance of the Romanian hero and the power of narratives of victimization in the creation of national fictions. Mary Poovey, an American cultural critic, summed up some of these issues for us very helpfully when she in effect set us an agenda for further work. Did historically specific nationalisms, she asked, whether state-produced or not, contribute to the normalization of an interiority constituted as trans-individual? Was this interiority gendered? Was it constituted as self-contradictory? How does it exist alongside that constituted by the family? What role does racial difference play in these narratives and what role does history writing play in constituting and reproducing this interiority? To all of this we could offer no easy answers but formulating the questions seemed to all of us to offer ways forward.

Our discussions circled around a number of tricky theoretical issues. Not surprisingly, the difficult questions for historians associated with the theoretical impact of poststructuralism occupied a prominent place. How is it possible to bring together textual analysis, with the insights it gives us into the 'ideological work' (Mary Poovey's term) and cultural logic of particular formations of national identity, with the everyday struggles of the illiterate and the excluded to constitute themselves as part of the nation? What is clear is that we need all the tools we have at our disposal and happily the atmosphere at Bellagio was one which did not privilege one kind of work or one kind of theoretical framework as against another. The presence of some sociologists encouraged us to think comparatively – a discipline which is particularly helpful for historians with their love of their 'own' period, their 'own' case-study, while the range of geographical areas we attempted to discuss, though obviously severely limited, helped us not to fall into the trap of treating the specific as the general.

One thing that was fascinating was the way in which the event acquired a life of its own – over three days of collective work it was possible to generate debate which went beyond any individual's contribution. This made it a genuinely exciting occasion and one which underlined for me how important *talk* is to thinking through intellectual and political issues. It was an enormous privilege to have the time and the space to put our minds together, to pool our knowledges, to think collectively rather than individually. Something which feminists have always valued but which is difficult to maintain in the ways that we would like. There were no conclusions to draw from Bellagio, and much that was *not* talked about – as, for example, the kinds of national identities which have been available for lesbians and gays – but it was energizing to know how much work is going on in these areas, to realise how interconnected are our efforts to formulate the questions, to do some of the necessary work to begin to answer them and to set ourselves some more.

Notes

Catherine Hall is a member of the *Feminist Review* collective and of the *Gender and History* collective. She is a Reader in Cultural Studies at the University of East London, the co-author with Leonore Davidoff of *Family Fortunes: Men and Women of the English Middle Class 1780–1850* (Hutchinson, 1987) and the author of *White, Male and Middle Class: Explorations in Feminism and History* (Polity, 1992).

1 A collection of papers from the symposium will be published in *Gender and History* Vol. 5, No. 2 (Summer) 1993.

References

ANDERSON, Benedict (1983) *Imagined Communities. Reflections on the Origin and Spread of Nationalism* London: Verso.

CULTURE OR CITIZENSHIP? Notes from the 'Gender and Colonialism' Conference, Galway, Ireland, May 1992

Clara Connolly

Galway, on the western seaboard of Ireland, was an intriguing venue for such a conference: on the edge of Europe, during a referendum campaign on Maastricht that turned on a discussion of the rights of citizenship for Irish women, in a successful nation-state, formed out of anti-colonial struggle, with an unresolved 'national question' festering on its disputed border; in a thriving cultural centre that some would argue presents a challenge to the liberal metropolitans of Dublin. The remarkable hospitality of the conference organizers, combined with the unexpected brilliance of the weather, turned the four days into a festival, with fringe and social events at least as memorable as the conference business itself.

Although the conference advertized itself as 'interdisciplinary' (under the auspices of the newly established Women's Studies Centre in University College, Galway), in fact, literary/cultural approaches, rather than those drawn from political economy or history, were most in evidence. There were 300 attenders, mainly from academic institutions in the British Isles, with some also from Canada and the US. In all there were eighty papers presented (with, apparently, many more offered) – a strong indication of the growing popularity of colonial and postcolonial studies. Fanon and Derrida were much-quoted authorities; the themes and many of the personalities from the *Oxford Literary Review* issue on neo-colonialism (1991) predominated.

There were four plenary sessions. The opening lecture was given by Barbara Harlow (University of Texas, author of *Resistance Literature*, 1987). The 'occupied territories' of her title were Ireland, Palestine, Texas – she drew on prison and insurgent writings from the Sinn Fein Women's Department, the PLO and Chicano writers in the US. Her political support for these movements was refreshingly direct – no fashionable suspicion of 'grand narratives' here. For example, she

'Feminists Against a Landscape', Connemara

attacked the recent wave of Irish 'revisionist' (or anti-nationalist) historians in a memorable phrase as 'the strip-searchers of academia'. This set the note for the majority of at least the Irish contributors to the conference – a clear pro-republican stance, opposed equally to the 'bourgeois nationalism' of the Irish state, and to the 'liberal revisionists'. There was little room here for gender issues, let alone for a feminist agenda.[1]

In the second plenary session, the speaker was Terry Eagleton, recently appointed Professor of English at Oxford, but perhaps better known in Ireland for his role in the cultural-nationalist project, Field Day. He reclaimed the Irishness of Oscar Wilde, representing his role of sexual transgressor as (at least partly) a protest against the rigidities of British imperialist culture.

The third plenary session was originally planned as a lecture from Homi Bhabha (editor of *Nation and Narration*, 1990). He was unable to attend, so instead there was a panel of speakers, and an open forum. The Chair set the context for discussion as a revisionist wave in Southern Ireland coinciding with the renewal of the Northern Irish conflict; the evasion by intellectuals of republican socialism; and the positioning of feminism in opposition to nationalism. Liz Curtis (author of *The Roots of Anti-Irish Racism*, 1984) referred to the cultural revival occurring in

West Belfast, Derry and Galway, ignored or down-played by the Dublin-based media. 'The nationalist community in the North', she said, 'feels abandoned.' Clair Wills[2] placed Ireland between the 'First' and 'Third' Worlds; she referred to the 'failed Enlightenment' in Ireland, where the distinction between 'public' and 'private' remains different from the rest of Europe. David Lloyd argued that although there was no clear distinction between the defence of ethnic identity and the struggle for political rights, a concentration on civil rights involved 'the erasure of certain kinds of community'. He referred to Carole Pateman's attack, in the US context, on a male-defined concept of citizenship, which ignores sexual difference. Luke Gibbons contrasted those forms of nationalism mobilized outside the state – particularly its cultural forms – with the political and economic struggles of the state. Economically, he argued, Ireland is a Third World country, but its 'cultural capital' is among the highest in the world. Its laws may enshrine reactionary, even clericalist positions, but the 'civic spirit' inherited from anti-colonial struggle renders them unenforceable.

The ensuing discussion was lively; it presented the first real opportunity for participants to engage in dialogue, since there was little time for discussion after the presentation of papers in the mini-sessions. I'll take up some of the themes later on, when I shall try to pull together the elements of a challenge to these views.

The final plenary session – a lecture by Gayatri Chakravorty Spivak (author of *In Other Worlds*, 1987) – was in marked contrast to the other three, firstly because it focused centrally on gender issues, and secondly because her main emphasis on this occasion was not on cultural theory, but on political economy.

The central gender issue in contemporary colonialism, she argued, is the position of homeworkers and out-workers, 87 per cent of them women. Caught between the private space of gendering and the international space of capitalism, they have no access to the protection offered by the state public sphere. She referred to the ways in which the New World Order has dismantled welfare socialism, and has led to the massive casualization of women's labour. She defined 'gendering' as 'internalized constraint working as choice': many such women, she argued, do not perceive their experience as oppression, they are, culturally, 'more at home at home' because of the masculinization of more socialized forms of labour in the factory, and they take a pride in their job because of the tradition of achieving fulfilment through domestic servitude. Gendering produces the most acute moral dilemmas: 'it is not just the European', she said, 'who universalizes the singular'.

The problem she posed was how to win such women to the public sphere: it is not enough to 'make good the laws first' and worry about 'interference with gendering' afterwards. 'We have to find ways of using *kinship* structures', she argued, 'to produce knowledge of *international* structures'. She referred with sympathy to the recent dilemma of Algerian feminists, reluctantly in support of a government-led coup against the Islamic Salvation Front, because the alternative would have been 'a war against women'. But how can they win the support of rural women 'who have been kept away from cultural imperialism for the wrong reasons'? The example of Algeria was particularly apt, because of the many references during the conference to Fanon's 'Algeria unveiled' (1959), with its opposition between the French imperialists' attempts to 'liberate' Algerian women, and the heroic role they played in the nationalist movement.

The experience of the plenary sessions was common to all of us, but the seminar sessions (with three/four papers in each) were many and varied. They were divided into roughly 'spatial' strands – imperial Britain, Ireland, India, Canada, Australia and Africa (mainly South Africa). There were also some thematically based sessions, on travel writing, 'Mapping the colonial body', and 'Theorizing colonialism and gender'. One's experience of the conference depended on either 'dipping in', or following a particular strand throughout. I followed the Irish strand – on the whole the best attended and the most polemical, fired as it was with a cultural revivalist mission. What I found was reflected in some (not all) of the other sessions, according to women who attended them – an attack on Enlightenment values, corrupted by colonialism, in the name of cultural difference.

A paper by Carol Coulter (Irish journalist and author of *Ireland Between the First and Third Worlds*, 1990) was unrepresentative only in its focus on politics rather than literature. She argued that the humanist concept of individual autonomy 'aborted' by imperialism was further distorted in postcolonial countries by cultural imperialism, and by international capitalism in reducing the concept of 'choice' to the market. In postcolonial countries, she outlined a common experience of rule by a metropolitan-educated middle-management caste: old communal patterns are broken down, creating only new forms of poverty. This produces a nostalgia for the extended family, and promotes a conservative nationalism fed on pre-capitalist communalist ideas. She compared Rana Kabbani (author of *Letter to Christendom*, 1989) with Desmond Fennell (Irish journalist who fulminates against 'the dehumanization of modern life promoted by feminists'), pointing to their common core, in spite of their differences, in a commitment to communal values, against those of Western feminism. She reserved her wrath for the 'liberal Ayatollahs' of Dublin and London, like Conor Cruise O'Brien and Fay Weldon. Feminists, she warned, must take as their starting point the colonial history of Ireland: they ignore the strengths of an appeal to communal values (a refuge against colonialism) at their peril.

This seemed particularly inappropriate to me in the context of an Ireland convulsed by the implications of the 'X' case. (In February 1992 a fourteen-year-old girl, pregnant as a result of rape, and taken by her parents to England for an abortion, was forced instead to return by an Irish High Court injunction. This decision was overturned by the Supreme Court, as a result of unprecedented public protest. The story is compellingly told by Ailbhe Smyth in her introduction to the *Abortion*

Papers: Ireland, 1992). In our guesthouses over the four days, we heard endless radio debates about the rights of women and the meaning of 'choice'. Abortion was being discussed, unprecedentedly in Ireland, in these terms. During the first day of the conference, we heard of a woman arrested for having a copy of the *Guardian*, which had been seized at Dublin Airport that morning because it carried an advertisement for an abortion clinic. But the next day we heard a left-wing TD (MP) exploit parliamentary privilege by reading on air the full advertisement, including the telephone number of the clinic. There seemed to be an explosion of open debate which was certainly new to me, having returned only for short visits since leaving Ireland in the mid-seventies.

And indeed, it culminated later in the year with a referendum result on abortion which had been campaigned for only by the 'pro-choice' groups – 'yes' to freedom of travel and information, 'no' to the right of abortion, offered under more restrictive terms than the Supreme Court judgement allowed. So, by default, abortion remains legal in some circumstances. A recent survey of members of the Irish Countrywoman's Association, a conservative rural-based organization, illustrates that 'a dramatic change has now taken place in the public attitude towards abortion, especially among women' (WAF, 1992: 7). After all, it has been a good year for Irish women.

I'm sure that Carol Coulter welcomes that result as much as I do, but how could she have missed the electric atmosphere in the country, and its relevance to her subject? In her eagerness to tar the 'modernizing liberals' (including feminists?) and the 'bourgeois nationalists' with the same brush, she has allowed her judgement to be clouded. The conservative communalism she asked us to note is not just an element of disaffected protest, to be provoked by feminists. It is enshrined since 1937 in the Constitution of the State. The caste of 'bourgeois national-ists', far from colluding with cultural imperialism to create the abstract citizen, was denying the female half of the population some of their most basic civil rights (to travel and information) in order to preserve 'the Irish way of life'. And the rights to which feminists and others appealed so effectively were those conveyed by membership of the European Community, not of the Irish nation. In the shadow of an EC referendum, the concept of 'citizenship' took on a clearly defined meaning, with implications for the everyday lives of Irish women.

In the plenary forum Avtar Brah (contributor to *'Race', Culture and Difference*, 1992) introduced another issue which brings the meaning of 'citizenship' to life; she asked where the Irish stood in relation to the question of 'race'. It is simply not good enough for the Irish left to trade on their anti-colonial credentials, and to identify themselves 'culturally' with the Third World. As Spivak reminds us, contemporary colonialism takes new forms, and Ireland is now decisively placed in the European trading block, one of the three (with the US and Japan) that dominate the world. On its own, it is far less poor than most countries of Eastern Europe, let alone in Africa and South America. What role will Ireland play in Fortress Europe, in protecting the diminishing right of refuge, and in fighting for citizenship rights (of the kind that Irish women insisted on) for the millions of 'third country nationals' in the EC? The fact that immigration controls have been tightened up at Shannon and Dublin airports (the backdoor to Europe) was not a subject of debate – even on the Irish left – during the Maastricht referendum campaign.

It seems to me that one of the best ways, still, to expose the limitations of the Enlightenment legacy is to turn its universalist concepts against itself, on its home ground. That's what Fanon was doing forty years ago. To expose the contradictions of a history-laden humanism imbued with Eurocentric masculine values, in the name of an oppressed or excluded group, is not the same thing as rejecting Enlightenment values altogether. As Laura Chrisman points out, 'white European occupation of the Subject position says everything about how power operates, but nothing "essential" to the concept of the Human Subject itself' (1993).

It is not clear how far the rejection of humanism goes on the part of the Galway speakers. Some are aware that the legacy of the Enlightenment includes dissident (socialist, feminist, anti-racist) perspectives, as well as more mainstream 'liberal' ones. David Lloyd, for example, in his essay in the 'Neo-colonialism' issue of the *Oxford Literary Review*, points to the 'spatial' terms under which 'the anti-racist cultural politics of the last decade has been expressed', and declares that it is not his intention to 'critique' these categories, merely to 'supplement' them 'by an analysis of the temporal axis which is equally constitutive of racist discourse' (1991: 63). He is careful to suggest that his work, on the 'normative developmental schema' of Western post-Enlightenment discourse on culture, is not intended to *replace* an anti-racist politics based on 'rights'. But Luke Gibbons at one point in the conference dismissed the concept of citizenship as 'a form of ethnocide', and David Lloyd echoed these sentiments, more cautiously, in his comments at the plenary forum (see page 106). This seems to me to be throwing out rather too much with the bathwater, especially when replacing it only with the equally abstract concept of 'difference'. In a careful consideration of the limits of individualism, Anne Phillips asks the poignant question, 'If we were to give up notions of abstract humanity, what if anything would take its place?' (1991: 55). We know that all over the contemporary world, these notions are being replaced by the most frightening forms of communalism, and 'difference'-based ethnic exclusivism. In that scenario, women are merely the property of the group, the symbol of the nation's future, to be protected or defiled according to their 'belonging'. The concept of equality enshrined in 'citizenship' offers more to women than that.

With an unresolved national war in the North, it is inevitable that the issue of nationalism would be an important focus of political activity in Ireland. It is true also that the *Field Day Anthology of Irish Writing*, with which Luke Gibbons and other Galway speakers are associated, is an ambitious attempt to forge an inclusive national identity, to which all communities on the island can belong. Luke Gibbons's essay in the

'Neo-colonialism' issue of the *Oxford Literary Review* contributes to the creation of a more generous and open future, by distinguishing between the more and the less racist elements of the nationalist tradition of the past. But an *exclusive* focus on the creation of a national identity confines 'culture' to its narrowest definition of 'ethnicity', and prevents the possibility of addressing other divisions in Irish society, at least as significant, such as those created by class and gender. An exclusive focus on colonialism and its effects – in other words on Ireland's relations with *Britain* – prevents the possibility of addressing the crucial question of Ireland's role in Europe and in the wider world.

Notes

Clara Connolly works at the Commission for Racial Equality in London. She is a member of the *Feminist Review* Editorial Collective and of the Irish Women's Abortion Support Group.

My warm thanks to friends in Galway and Dublin, who made my visit to Ireland so stimulating and enjoyable.

1 However, there were some excellent feminist papers, two of which, by Nash and Thapar, are published in this issue, and others will appear in future. A book of the conference is planned by the organizers, to be published by Routledge. A second conference on the theme will be held at Galway in Spring 1994.
2 Clair Wills, David Lloyd and Luke Gibbons are all authors in the Neo-colonialism issue of the *Oxford Literary Review*.

References

BHABHA, Homi (1990) editor, *Nation and Narration* London: Routledge.

BRAH, Avtar (1992) 'Difference, diversity and differentiation' in DONALD and RATTANSI (1992).

CHRISMAN, Laura (1993) 'Theorizing race, racism and culture: pitfalls of idealist tendencies' *Paragraph* Vol. 16, No. 1, Edinburgh University Press.

COULTER, Carol (1990) *Ireland Between the First and Third Worlds* Dublin: Attic Press.

CURTIS, Liz (1984) *Nothing But the Same Old Story: the Roots of Anti-Irish Racism* London: Information on Ireland.

DEANE, Seamus (1991) editor, *The Field Day Anthology of Irish Writing* Derry: Field Day Publications.

DONALD, J. and RATTANSI, A. (1992) editors, *'Race' Culture and Difference* London: Sage.

FANON, Frantz (1959) 'Algeria unveiled', in FANON (1989).

—— (1989) *Studies in a Dying Colonialism* London: Earthscan.

GIBBONS, Luke (1991) 'Race against time: racial discourse and Irish history' *Oxford Literary Review* Vol. 13, Nos 1–2 (on neo-colonialism) 96–117.

HARLOW, Barbara (1987) *Resistance Literature* New York: Methuen.

KABBANI, Rana (1989) *Letter to Christendom* London: Virago.

LLOYD, David (1991) 'Race under representation' *Oxford Literary Review* Vol. 13, Nos 1–2 (on neo-colonialism) 63–94.

OSBORNE, Peter (1991) editor, *Socialism and the Limits of Liberalism* London: Verso.

PHILLIPS, Anne (1991) 'So what's wrong with the individual? Socialist and feminist debates on equality' in OSBORNE (1991).

SMYTH, Ailbhe (1992) editor, *The Abortion Papers: Ireland* Dublin: Attic Press.

SPIVAK, Gayatri (1987) *In Other Worlds: Essays in Cultural Politics* New York: Methuen.

WAF (1992) *Women Against Fundamentalism Journal* No. 4.

REVIEWS

The Politics of Truth
Michèle Barrett

Polity Press: Cambridge, 1992, 194 pp
ISBN 0 745 60503 6, £10.95 Pbk
ISBN 0 745 60502 8, £35.00 Hbk

This book is at once a textbook survey and critique of the theory of ideology, and the site of Michèle Barrett's settling of accounts with Marxism. With the honesty we have come to expect of her, she announces that she has now nailed her colours 'to the mast of a more general post-Marxism'. Foucault, despite some jitters about his competence, has been entrusted with the helm, and Laclau and Mouffe are prominent among the crew.

That the theory of ideology would prove the acid test of Barrett's commitments had already been signalled in her self-critical Introduction to the 1988 edition of *Women's Oppression Today* – where she remarks on the reliance of her argument on an unthought-through concept of 'gender ideology'. At that time, however, she was reluctant to dump an idea which still seemed a potentially fruitful tool to investigate the relationship of the psychic to the social. On further scrutiny, it has been rejected as inherently unhelpful. This is in part because of the equivocation between its neutral use to refer to 'historical consciousness', and its critical or epistemological

definition as involving a necessary element of illusion or distortion of the truth. But it is mainly because of its 'class belongingness': the mystification to which we are directed in its critical use is one which serves class interests and is explicable by reference to them. The theory of ideology thus rests an on explanatory model which is no longer – if it ever was – appropriate. For today, argues Barrett, it is only the dogmatist who thinks that social inequalities and political differences can be 'subsumed under or reduced to the question of class'.

In principle, this leaves open the possibility that 'ideology', conceived as 'mystification' accountable to multiple sources and serving complex interests (patriarchy, racism, nationalism), might still be salvaged. But given how closely Barrett associates the economic and class reductionism of Marxist theory with its realist epistemology, and her generally favourable commentary on Foucault, Derrida and others who have ditched that paradigm of knowledge, what in effect is being argued is that once you have broken with a class perspective there is very little mileage in the idea of a systematically sustained false consciousness about social reality at all.

On the other hand, despite her criticism of 'anti-humanism', Barrett has by no means shifted to any position which views experience or self-expression as guarantors of political correctness and 'authenticity'. Indeed, her support for Foucault means that her dismissal of economic determinism is conducted within a framework which is itself, arguably, just as vexed by the assumptions of determinism, albeit the 'agent' in the construction of the subject is now conceived as a generalized power rather than in terms of class interests. This makes for many unresolved areas of discussion in her book regarding the formation of subjectivity and our powers of self – and social – change (and, indeed, the directions these should take).

As one who has always resisted the use of the concept of ideology to plug rather than expound problems in social theory, I have an immediate sympathy with the critical purposes of this book, which offers a lucid assembly of arguments against which left intellectuals may test their own commitments in these uncertain times. Like Laclau and Mouffe, however, Barrett is reliant on a very circumscribed version of Marxism and fails sufficiently to attend to all that theory which in some sense remained nailed to the Marxist masthead, even as it criticized its reductive and class essentialist tendencies. It is regrettable, in this respect, that the book doesn't engage more with the work of Williams, Thompson, Frankfurt School, Sartre, 'critical realism' and other offerings, the status of whose argument seems to me to be very unclear in terms of the criteria deployed by Barrett for dividing between Marxism and post-Marxism.

Moreover, while she is incisive about the ways in which Gramsci and Althusser represent limit-to-breaking points for the coherence of Marxism, she is far less prepared to push at the implications of the many tensions she remarks on in the argument of the post-Marxists. For example, she nowhere takes the measure of her criticism of Laclau and Mouffe for reproducing the 'classical Marxist mind-set' of economy, then state, then ideology, then 'culture' in their discussion of the hegemonic transformation of the post-war social order; her defence of Foucault against the charge of relativism on the grounds that his work is brimful of truth claims seems beside the point if he holds a relativist position on truth itself; and while Barrett notes many ambiguities in Foucault's argument, she is rather soft on the role played in generating these by his unanchored notion of power.

To be fair, despite the option for Foucault, Barrett is much more confident about the need to go beyond Marx than about what to put in his place. Thus while those, hopefully not many, who can think only in terms of 'apostasy' may seize on her book as a definitive statement of position, it is really very tentative in its directives, and its reservation of judgement is perhaps its most notable feature.

Opinions will no doubt differ about the extent to which Barrett is here being judicious as opposed to evasive. If I have a quarrel with her book it is not that it hesitates to pronounce on which theory will finally emerge as adequate to our times, but that it is so scant in its discussion of the political aims or conceptions of progress and emancipation which might allow us to come to a decision in this respect. Whereas in the past Barrett's theoretical analysis has been closely related to an existing context of political activism, especially that within the feminist movement, her present book is academic by comparison, and is very veiled in its treatment of what she now regards to be the political priorities, whether of feminism, or of the left more generally. She says enough to persuade me that she is not now simply opting for some form of libertarian 'identity' politics, but not enough to make clear what other norms and goals she believes we can, and should, be seeking to realize. I think she would agree, however, that we can't get our theory right in a vacuum, and that it is impossible to make judgements about the sensitivity and strategic implications of social theory independently of consideration of what we want to achieve politically. Or if we are being invited to view all attempts to name

a truth in politics as misconceived, perhaps we shouldn't trade on the idea of a 'politics of truth' at all?

Kate Soper

Reference

BARRETT, M. (1988) *Women's Oppression Today: The Marxist-Feminist Encounter* London: Verso.

Lighting up the Screen: Feminism and Film

The Woman at the Keyhole: Feminism and Women's Cinema
Judith Mayne
Indiana University Press: Bloomington, Indiana, 1990
ISBN 0 253 20606 5, $12.95, £8.99 Pbk
ISBN 0 253 33719 4, $35 Hbk

Issues in Feminist Film Criticism
Edited by Patricia Erens
Indiana University Press: Bloomington, Indiana, 1991
ISBN 0 253 20610 3, $17.50, £12.50 Pbk
ISBN 0 253 31964 1, $45 Hbk

If you will excuse the irresistable pun, female spectatorship is one of the Mayne issues in feminist film criticism today. Patricia Erens's new collection, an overview of 1980s feminist work on film, and Judith Mayne's original and suggestive revision of theoretical knots in the history of feminist engagement with cinema, demonstrate clearly how much of a hold the problem of the female spectator has on the feminist imagination. Active or passive, masochistic or narcissistic, unified or dispersed, sociologically researched or theoretically postulated, the female gaze is beset by all the questions of female subjectivity plus those that the study of patriarchal

and commodified culture has brought in its train. Why should this be? Why privilege spectatorship over the analysis of text, institution or film's social and political functioning in the public sphere? Women's pleasure, it seems, is still an obscure object of desire.

Years ago, German film theorist Gertrud Koch posed the question of why women go to see men's films at all, if Laura Mulvey's analysis of the look in dominant cinema as intrinsically masculine was right, thus precluding female pleasure in film viewing. In response to Mulvey's pessimism also, Mary Ann Doane shifted her sights from men's film to the woman's film of the 1940s, and came up with an equivocal answer with women's pleasure hovering between masochism and narcissism. A recent collection by Philip Schlesinger *et al.* researches the experience of women viewing violence on TV and film; here, the term 'pleasure' does not figure anywhere. *Unpleasure* of the female spectator ('why am I watching this?') is, we might say, a more likely candidate for feminist analysis than its utopian or compromised counterpart. In popular cinema, the woman of the 1980s and 1990s, from *Fatal Attraction* to *Basic Instinct*, is brought face to face with her worst nightmares far more often than with her dreams.

In Erens's book, Robin Wood attributes this phenomenon to a 'massive retaliation' against femin-

ism on the part of Hollywood (p. 341).
One would expect then, that recent
feminist film criticism would engage
with this historically specific moment of misogyny (and homophobia)
in the production of popular culture,
but no such luck. Both Erens's selection of representative articles from
the 1980s and Judith Mayne's evolving theoretical and critical work
exhibit a concern with the female
spectator which is resolutely stuck in
accentuating the positive: the search
for female pleasure in women's films,
or a recuperation thereof in dominant cinema, if at all possible. By
default, this results in the reproduction of a by now familiar canon of
'women's cinema', which can roughly
be subdivided into the categories of
older movies (*Gentlemen Prefer
Blondes, Stella Dallas* again, *The
Big Sleep* again and the films of
Dorothy Arzner); avant-garde films
(Yvonne Rainer, Chantal Akerman,
Helke Sander) and more mainstream films with a pinch or, oc-
casionally, a good shot of feminism
thrown in (*I've Heard the Mermaids
Singing, A Question of Silence, Desperately Seeking Susan*). The absence, then, of the 1980s backlash
movies can be explained in large part
by a search for female tradition in
film-making and spectatorship, by
recuperative readings, and by the
turn to psychoanalytical and semio-
tic paradigms in film analysis at the
expense of more sociological, institutional and historical concerns.

This theoretical turn is well-
documented in Erens's collection and
exemplified in Judith Mayne's
critical engagement with the history
of feminist film criticism and theory.
Organized in three parts, addressing
spectacle and narrative, female
authorship, and early cinema in relation to women's films respectively,
The Woman at the Keyhole is constantly in dialogue with her theoretical foremothers. Laura Mulvey plays
a part in the first chapter which tries
to theorize the screen as a more
complex figure for cinematic spec-

tacle than Mulvey's deterministic
look. Claire Johnston's work on
Dorothy Arzner provides Mayne
with an opportunity for a subtle
critique, resulting in a promising
re-evaluation of issues of female
authorship and lesbian signature in
Arzner's oeuvre.

Mayne's exploration of the
'primitive' in 'primitive' (=early)
cinema draws on and questions
Linda Williams and Lucy Fischer's
re-examination of Meliès as well as
Burch, Gunning and other analysts
of early cinema. It is here, especially
in the final section on Trinh T. Minh
Ha's *Reassemblage* and Laleen Jaya-
manne's *A Song of Ceylon*, that
Mayne really begins to extend the
familiar paradigms of feminist film
theory into a novel and highly suggestive exploration of race and the
avant garde. Suggestions, however,
need following up, and Mayne's
largely intra-theoretical brand of
criticism does not as yet promise a
new direction for the 1990s in terms
of race, spectatorship and film-
making, badly needed though that is.

More surprisingly perhaps,
Erens's *Issues in Feminist Film
Criticism*, in its very diversity and
quantity of theoretical and critical
material, manages not to give much
serious attention to the female spectator of colour, whether implied or
empirical either. Jane Gaines's
'White privilege and looking relations: race and gender in feminist
film theory' (1986) is the sole representative of a developing body of
work on the racial look, and therefore carries the burden of absences
elsewhere. Her sophisticated reading of *Mahogany* combines issues of
production and the iconography of
the star (Diana Ross) with formal
analysis and a discussion of Black
history and politics in the US – such
a range of concerns is rare in this
collection. No wonder then that in
the end Gaines can do no more than
make a beginning in theorizing race
as a factor in cinematic language.

Yet it is an important beginning.

Without explicitly addressing questions of race, several other articles in Erens's anthology can be used in support of Gaines's attempt at a more complex view of cinematic language via the diversified look. In 'Rethinking women's cinema: aesthetics and feminist theory' (1987) Teresa de Lauretis offers a fascinating account of how film can construct and address a diverse audience in her analysis of Lizzie Borden's *Born in Flames*. And Jackie Stacey, in 'Desperately seeking difference' poses the question of women's desire for each other and its place in the theory of the look: 'Do all women have the same relationship to images of themselves?' (p. 368) In these examples, lesbian spectatorship and spectatorship of colour are aligned in a radical questioning of the premisses of both the male and 'the' female gaze.

While offering few new departures, *Issues in Feminist Film Criticism*, true to its stated programme of selection, presents at least a wide variety of approaches. Structured in four parts (Women and Representation, Rereading Hollywood, Critical Methodology: Feminist Filmmaking, and Assessing Films Directed by Women), it gives a good picture of the main debates in feminist film criticism over the past twenty years, even if on individual films the excitement of such debate is often lost in the tedium of repeated plot synopses and re-statement of previous critics' positions. The same is true of Erens's introductions to each part of the collection, which rather lazily cite bits from the articles themselves rather than provide an overview of the field under discussion.

Read in sequence, *Issues in Feminist Film Criticism* furthermore charts the aforementioned turn away from sociology ('positive images') to theoreticism and, later still, a self-reflective concern with spectatorship. While I doubt the need for yet another reprint of seventies pieces such as Mulvey's, and Johnston and Cook's article on Raoul Walsh, it is good to see many old favourites all together, as well as some new ones: B. Ruby Rich's 'Antiporn: soft issue, hard world', Tania Modleski on Hitchcock, Julia Lesage on feminist documentary filmmaking, Kaja Silverman's 'Disembodying the female voice', Jane Gaines on alternative pleasure, and Teresa de Lauretis and Jackie Stacey, as mentioned before.

But the largely missing issues are perhaps the main ones. In 'Illicit pleasures: feminist spectators and *Personal Best*', Elizabeth Ellsworth argues for the vital role that feminist film criticism has to play as an interpretive community of resistance to dominant cultural values. Her article is important because it focuses two issues absent in the rest of Erens's collection: (1) the notion of community which challenges the still all too common assumption that film viewing is a private affair of isolated individuals in the dark, rather than a social activity in which meaning is produced through a negotiation of personal experience/pleasure and public discourses; and (2) the notion of a feminist, as distinct from a female spectator *per se*. As I see it, feminist spectatorship is informed by a specific political consciousness which intersects with female pleasure but can quite easily be at odds with it too. The female gaze, as an empirical or theoretical entity, is not necessarily co-extensive with a feminist view of film. And since cinema is not just fantasy, but – perhaps paradoxically – also a particularly powerful form of legitimation of fantasy, it is all the more important for feminists to keep their political eyes peeled at the keyhole of what is still overwhelmingly a patriarchal, racist and homophobic cultural industry.

Maria Lauret

References

DOANE, Mary Ann (1984) 'The "woman's film": possession and address' in Mary Ann Doane *et al.*, (1984) editors, *Revision: Essays in Feminist Film Criticism* Los Angeles: American Film Institute: 67–82.

KOCH, Gertrud (1985) 'Why women go to men's films' in Gisela Ecker (1985) editor, *Feminist Aesthetics* London: Women's Press: 108–19.
SCHLESINGER, Philip *et al.* (1992) editors, *Women Viewing Violence* London: British Film Institute.

Inside/Out: Lesbian Theories, Gay Theories
Edited by Diana Fuss

Routledge: London, 1992
ISBN 4 159 0237 1, £12.99 Pbk
ISBN 0 415 90236 3, £40.00 Hbk

Underscoring *Inside/Out*, the latest title from Routledge, is the subheading 'lesbian theories, gay theories'; a separation between two communities is thus implied. In fact, and to the book's credit, neither its format nor its politics recognizes any such separation as its lesbian and gay contributors play in and out of others, and each other's, paradigms and conclusions. This is, as the flyleaf promises, work from the second wave of queer theory, with a determination to go beyond identity politics, though often using their essentialism as a starting point. Anti-essentialist while recognizing essentialism's seductions, one senses some anxiety as to where politics might go 'post-identity'. A particular problem, as Diana Fuss points out in her excellent introduction, is how to retain a notion of alterity (that we, as homosexuals, are different from and in opposition to the paradigm of compulsory heterosexuality) without resorting to simple binaries which assert difference at the expense of any correspondence, since, 'Every outside is also an alongside' (p. 5). The politics she proposes is a chameleon one where identity is more performance than epistemology, continually posed then called into question, 'less a matter of final discovery than perpetual reinvention' (p. 7). Inside/outside, homosexual/heterosexual, Fuss argues for

the deconstruction of such categories, asking, what gets left out of these by now well-established binaries which continue to present, 'an opposition which could at least plausibly be said to secure its seemingly inviolable dialectical structure only by assimilating and internalizing other sexualities . . . to its own rigid polar logic' (p. 2). Her point is convincingly argued though it could be said that she misses the opportunity for a more effective destabilization of the heterosexual/homosexual binary in failing to follow through her remark about what we might call, the 'queerly queer'. These days this is an expansive category, representing not only the bisexuals, the transvestites, and the transsexuals whom her category invokes and who have always had a problematic relation to the homosexual community, but also the daddy boys, the politically queer and the lesbians who sleep with men who re-present themselves as a colourful and contentious part of the contemporary lesbian and gay scene.

In itself the book is well centred in that it combines a traditional literary and film criticism with a theoretical intentionality that is always at some point concerned to ally itself with a contemporary politic. The sections devoted specifically to activism foreground such concerns, but most of the essays begin out of a specific historical situation. Of course, this combination engenders its own issues and debates. The question of the colonization of AIDS work by the academy is raised in Thomas Yingling's 'AIDS in America: postmodern governance, identity and experience' where AIDS is explored, amongst other things, as a technology of production and re-production in relation to an AIDS archive that is already too vast for a single reader/researcher to absorb. In Jeff Nunokawa's, '"All the sad young men": AIDS and the work of mourning', AIDS is analyzed as liter-ary conceit and as metaphor, re-establishing the link between text and world text, a link which Cindy Patton in 'Visualizing safe sex' takes up at the point where 'pedagogy and pornography collide'.

Each essay is then dedicated in its intention to intersect theory with politics and each is to varying de-grees successful. Still, at some point the question that needs to be asked by any reader is, where do we go from here? How do we take the essays and the theories and the thesis out of the book and back into the community? It is a question which Ed Cohen asks in relation to the academy; how should 'we', as theorists, academics, students, situated both inside and out of the academy formulate and contribute to (should we even want

to?) a lesbian and gay studies pro-gramme? It is the question women's studies has had to ask itself, is still asking itself, or in some cases, has stopped asking itself – absorption or ghettoization, how much of the choice is even ours? The debate is as pressing in Britain where resource centres and courses are just begin-ning to be established as it continues to be in the US where resources are more extensive but the homophobic backlash against such advance-ments is more vituperative. It is a question the book takes up but does not really answer, preferring per-haps to leave conclusions to the reader.

On the whole, however, the book is an excellent introduction to some of the very best in contemporary lesbian and gay theory, committed, versatile and self-critical. Thanks to the current publishing vogue in queer theory (a phenomenon subject to its own speculation and irony) it will, almost certainly, not be the last.

Clare Whatling

Polish Women, Solidarity and Feminism
Anna Reading
Macmillan: London, 1992
ISBN 0 333 55063 3
£47.50 Hbk

This book is the product of a Western feminist's collision with Polish cul-tural reality and an attempt to understand that reality. It is also a record of a personal voyage of dis-covery. The structure of the book mirrors this process of approxi-mation – as the author puts it: mov-ing from the perception of an out-sider (someone beyond the fixed boundary/*granica*) to a position of more tentative inclusion (within shifting borders/*kresy*). Thus, the first section comprises material

culled from existing 'accounts' of women's position in Polish culture and society, while the second, larger section gives voice to Polish women themselves. The picture of subordi-nation and oppression painted at the outset becomes more nuanced as women themselves speak about their lives. The final section of the book offers the most detailed account to date of the various feminist groups which have recently come into exist-ence.

The book has much to offer. First, it draws an uncompromising picture of the sexism which satu-rates Polish culture – historically, linguistically, socially and in litera-ture; under state socialism and in Solidarity. The author's linguistic and literary insights and references

are of particular value here. For example, she makes interesting links between nationalism and the position of women and illustrates this with the observation made by the writer Czesław Miłosz concerning the 'feminine invasion' of literature during the periods of Polish history when nationalism took a back seat. Second, considerable space is devoted to interviews with women themselves. Reading is thus attempting to puncture the systematic silence which has existed around gender issues, and at the same time allow women a valid voice as women. There are some real gems in the interviews here. One example is the conversation with the economics graduate who now manages a Sex and Gun shop in Łódź.
Question: 'Could you tell me how you came to be interested in sex shops and why you wanted to run one?' Answer: 'Everything in Poland now is returning to normal. We're to be a part of Europe. . .' To cap it all, the shop, with its telling combination of merchandise, has special financial concessions from the city council.

A deeply sexist culture is undoubtedly a vital dimension influencing the position of women in Polish society, and an area which has been hardly studied at all. But the question the book sets out to answer – What does the fall of communism mean for Polish women? – cannot be answered in these terms alone: the specific distinguishing characteristics of state socialism as a political system have to be taken into account. All we need do is look at how women all over the Eastern bloc, regardless of national culture, regardless of the strength of the established Church, are experiencing a similar de-gradation of social position, just as the 'conditions' of life are set to become 'easier'. Similarly, the fact there has been a general lack of interest in feminism across Eastern Europe cannot really be explained in terms of the content of a single nation's culture. And here we

are confronted with the fascinating and important question which emerges from the pages of Anna Reading's book: How can a culture be so rampantly sexist, and yet have been accompanied by such systematic rejection of feminism? Culture and tradition *are* important, but one cannot assume that these are re-created in the same way in state socialism as in liberal capitalism.

In this book, state socialism is termed 'state capitalism', that is to say, it is conflated with Western capitalism because 'women are instruments of labour, as under capitalism and they are other/unknowable, as under capitalism' (p. 38). Elsewhere: 'Poland's economy displayed the same contradictions as economies in the capitalist West – competition, accumulation and exploitation. There were and are in both East and West those who sell their labour to those (owners) in control' (p. 6). This equation is quite misleading; it ignores the specific importance of private property and civil society in shaping gender relations. If differences of political system count for little in this explanatory framework, then the shift from one system to the other must also be essentially meaning*less*, a conclusion which I would contest. A focus on culture means that while Reading mines the subtleties of sexism in the Polish language, the opportunity to examine the nuances of other, more politically based, meanings is missed. What does it mean, for example, to be a 'second-class citizen' (p. 61), or a first-class citizen come to that, under a political system where there is no civil society? Only by looking at culture *and* the specifics of political domination in Eastern Europe, I suggest, is it possible to explain the very contradictory, and often self-contradictory accounts which women give of themselves in the second part of this book.

Peggy Watson

Dimensions of Radical Democracy

Edited by Chantal Mouffe

Verso: London, 1992
ISBN 0 860 91556 5, £11.95 Pbk
ISBN 0 860 91344 9, £34.95 Hbk

Engendering Democracy

Anne Phillips

Polity Press: Cambridge, 1991
ISBN 0 745 60649 0, £10.95 Pbk
ISBN 0 745 60648 2, £35.00 Hbk

The task of rethinking democratic politics is, Chantal Mouffe asserts, 'more urgent than ever'. She is not alone in her sense of urgency – it is to be found in the writings of conservatives and feminists, liberals and postmodernists alike. All seem to be clamouring to rework democratic principles within their own theoretical perspectives and lay claim to the concept as their own. Democracy is the issue of the moment; institutions are being restructured, concepts are being reworked. This is so not only for those countries undergoing a process of 'democratization', but also for those which pride themselves on their long tradition as democratic states. Yet, amongst all the rhetoric about democracy there exists no cohesive sense of what it is to be democratic. We may all be democrats now, but are we all the same sort of democrat?

It is in this context that Anne Phillips's book *Engendering Democracy* and Chantal Mouffe's collection *Dimensions of Radical Democracy* engage with a vibrant and topical debate. 'The task of the left', states Mouffe, 'should be the extension and deepening of the democratic revolution initiated two hundred years ago.' Meanwhile Anne Phillips argues that democracy should be rethought with gender written in.

These attempts to rethink democracy from socialist and feminist perspectives add to the debate raging between libertarians and communitarians, anti-foundationalists and poststructuralists, regarding how best to construct a democratic theory, free of the faults of the liberal model. The existence of such numerous critiques of liberal democracy is certainly not new. What is novel, however, is the extent to which current oppositional stances aspire not to reject all that liberalism values (as has been the case in much Marxist and some feminist writing) but to force liberal democratic societies to be accountable for their professed ideals. The dominant concern seems to have become the revelation of the radical future of liberal structures. For there is a wary recognition, amongst many who have long denied it, that socialist goals can only be achieved in any acceptable way within a liberal democratic regime.

What is sought then, is not the demise of all liberal values and structures, but liberalism freed from its individualistic and rationalistic fetters. It is this project that is manifest in the work of both Anne Phillips and Chantal Mouffe.

Mouffe's *Dimensions of Radical Democracy* contains a wide-ranging, inspired and yet prudent collection of essays; addressing the issues of citizenship, pluralism, community and justice; drawing on contributors from France, Britain, America, Canada and Slovenia; representing the fascinating diversity of the contemporary state of debate. What distinguishes the contributors to this collection (who include Jean Leca, Bryan Turner, Mary Dietz, Michael Walzer, Kirstie McClure, Louise Marcil-Lacoste, Maurizio Passerin d'Entrèves, Etienne Tassin, Slavoj Žižek, Quentin Skinner and Sheldon Wolin) from traditional liberal theorists of democracy is the association of democracy with community and citizenship; an understanding that citizenship involves thinking from a position of commonality and is in some sense incompatible with an individualistic framework. I cannot hope to engage with all the issues raised here, and instead focus upon only those pieces which impact on the debates addressed by Phillips – those of Dietz, Passerin d'Entrèves and Mouffe. The project common to these writers is to theorize a form of pluralism which values equality, and a form of democracy which actually operates to undermine structural oppression and encourage participation.

'How', asks Mouffe, 'can we defend the gains of the democratic revolution and acknowledge the constitutive role of liberalism in the emergence of a pluralistic democracy, while trying to redress the negative consequences of individualism?' The liberal version allows for only an instrumental community, a community in which individuals with previously defined interests and identities enter in view of furthering those interests. The civic republican community, on the other hand, requires a single substantive idea of the common good. Liberalism reduces the citizenship to a mere legal status, civic republicanism emphasizes the value of political participation and attributes a central role to our insertion in a political community. 'The problem', claims Mouffe, 'is not that of replacing one tradition by the other but drawing on both and trying to combine their insights in a new conception of citizenship adequate for a project of radical and plural democracy.'

What is being advocated here is a form of pluralism which works within limits. As such it is distinct from certain forms of 'postmodern' politics which emphasize heterogeneity and valorize all difference. For, as Mouffe convincingly argues, in order that pluralism be compatible with the struggle against inequality, one must be able to discriminate between differences that exist but should not exist, and differences that do not exist but should exist. Any such criteria, claims Mouffe, cannot be provided by either traditional liberal pluralists or by

the recent forms of postmodern exaltation of difference.

In the midst of this battle over conceptions of citizenship, we find an increasing number of theorists, Maurizio Passerin d'Entrèves amongst them, turning to the work of Hannah Arendt for inspiration. For Arendt the constitution of public spaces of action depends on the existence of a space of appearance; spaces which are created every time individuals gather together politically and therefore not restricted to a set of institutions or a specific location. It disappears the moment the discussion ceases and is therefore always a potential space. By establishing a space between individuals, an in-between which connects and separates them at the same time, the world provides the physical context within which political action can arise.

Hence Arendt places stress on the artificiality of politics – a creation of speech and action, not the result of some natural or innate trait shared by all human beings. She therefore rejects appeals to 'identity' as the basis for political community. One's ethnic, religious, racial or gender identity is irrelevant to one's role as a citizen and should never be the basis of membership in the political community. Furthermore, according to Arendt the search for intimacy is characteristic of those groups excluded from the public realm. Such intimacy is bought at the price of worldlessness which is 'always a form of barbarism'. Ties of intimacy and warmth can never become political.

It is interesting to contrast such a perspective, admittedly idiosyncratic but gaining increasing attention of late, with current feminist writings on democracy and citizenship. Carol Gilligan, for example – the focus of Mary Dietz's critique – has argued that there is a feminist 'ethics of care' which promotes values based on the experiences of women (such as the experience of motherhood in the private realm) as opposed to a male liberal 'ethics of justice'. Arendt would probably have agreed; the difference lies in the evaluation of such development. For Gilligan, recognition of this phenomenon involves a revaluation of these different ethics and a celebration of the female; for Arendt it is not clear that it entails anything more than the containment of the influence of the private.

Dietz rejects Gilligan's 'maternal thinking' and the argument that motherhood should provide the model for a new type of politics and citizenship. A democratic politics, she argues echoing Arendt, is linked to the existence of a public sphere where people act as citizens. This acting cannot be fashioned on the type of initimate bond that exists between mother and child. 'It is true', states Dietz, 'that the modern category of the citizen has been constructed in a way that, under the pretence of universality, postulated a homogeneous public, which relegated all particularity and difference to the private, and that it has contributed to the exclusion of women. But that does not mean that the answer is to introduce women's so-called specific tasks into the very definition of citizenship.' Although the distinction between public and private is problematic, we should not reject the distinction. 'What we need', argues Dietz, 'is a new way of understanding the nature of the private and of the public, as well as a different mode of articulation between them.' And in this she is not alone – as Carole Pateman has stated: 'The dichotomy between the private and the public is central to almost two centuries of feminist writing and political struggle; it is, ultimately, what the feminist movement is all about.'

It is then, no great surprise that the two key areas of exploration addressed by Phillips are the need to develop mechanisms of representative democracy that explicitly ac-

knowledge gender difference and inequality, and to reorder the relationship between public and private spheres such that the distinction loses its gendered quality. The former is a short-term tactic (a sort of affirmative action programme to rectify previous inequalities); the latter is a long-term aim. What we therefore find is the assertion of sexual difference within political structures as a mechanism for achieving its longer term political irrelevance. This seeming paradox is not specific to the writing of Phillips (who acknowledges and accepts the paradox as such within her writing). It haunts the debate and thinking of many feminist agendas. The paradox is such that when Mouffe states that; 'gender should be irrelevant to the practice of citizenship', we do not know whether she is at odds or at one with Phillips.

If it is the case that the historical division of the social into the public and private spheres, the location of politics within the public and the exclusion of women from this realm, have all worked to underpin the development of a theoretical understanding of democracy and citizenship that are male-defined, what theoretical moves should we now make to rectify this state of affairs? Develop a non-gendered conception of citizenship; challenge the bifurcation of society into public and private spheres; redraw the boundary; assert a 'female perspective' in a newly conceived form of political practice.... Even if we accept the diagnosis, there is little agreement on the remedy. Mouffe calls for a non-gendered conception of citizenship; Phillips for a rethinking of democracy with gender written in.

The fear, so prevalent now, is that to manifest a concern about the presence of women in political institutions and processes is to assert an essentialist assumption that women will automatically speak for women, represent all women in some way. Yet if we reject such an assumption, we must consider whether we are left claiming that the actual gender of those engaged in institutional politics is irrelevant to our concerns as feminists.

What is interesting in this development, is that if we distance ourselves from the assertion that there is a 'women's perspective' which we seek to introduce into politics, we are left simply asserting the importance of numerical equity: in other words, the anti-essentialist theorizing of poststructuralism takes us back to a liberal agenda. Unless, that is, we retain the materialist standpoint position that difference can be contingent rather than essential, but is none the less politically important for that.

In this context, Phillips clearly emphasizes that participatory forms of democratic politics have long been central to feminist practice. Throughout second-wave American feminism, the movement has been informed by democratic organization and practice – spontaneous gatherings and marches, diverse action groups, face-to-face assemblies, consensus decision-making. The women's movement, comments Phillips, took participation 'almost as its definition of democracy'. Thus there is a tradition of participatory democracy which exists within feminism, a tradition to which we can appeal in the current attempts to theorize a democracy based upon active citizenship.

Thus our ambition should be to reconceive and reconstruct the existing division between public and private spheres of life, conscious of the implications this will have for women's political participation, not in the expectation that this participation will remain distinct in form but in the hope that it will become more integral to a newly revitalized political arena.

The writing of Phillips and the above-mentioned contributors to the Mouffe collection add significantly to this debate on democratization and are invaluable reading for all who wish to ponder how we, as feminists, might engage with it.

Judith Squires

Destabilizing Theory: Contemporary Feminist Debates
Edited by Michèle Barrett and Anne Phillips
Polity Press: Cambridge, 1992
ISBN 0 745 60794 0, £11.95 Pbk
ISBN 0 745 60794 2, £45.00 Hbk

What a feast: a specially commissioned collection of papers, all new bar one, and that one revised, from feminists working in Britain, Australia and the United States reflecting on similar questions from their own disciplinary locations in the humanities and social sciences. As readers of this journal know, unitary conceptions of feminist theory or feminist interests have been blown apart by the politics of difference and by all those trends that are subsumed under the rather ambiguous label of postmodernism. Indeed some of the key debates of the last two decades that have led to the current instability have been in this very journal.

One of the aims of this collection is to reflect on the gulf that now seems to yawn between the feminist theory of the 1970s and the theories of the 1990s. Reading the editors' introduction is a salutary reminder of how the language of feminism – as well as the politics – has changed over these two decades. Questions of meaning, identity, representation, difference, are now the subject of debate rather than older preoccupations about social structures, production and reproduction, domestic labour and so on. Is bridging the gap between these languages, between the different political projects of the 1970s and 1990s possible? Is it even a desirable aim? Should we see the changed agenda of feminism as an advance on earlier debates, or as a distraction from our earlier certainties about our aims and political agenda? Does the focus on difference and heterogeneity deflect attention from systematic and structured inequalities? In posing these and other questions *Destabilizing Theory* is a valuable contribution to the growing literature about the possibility of a specifically feminist epistemology. Have we anything general left to say?

These are vexed and challenging questions and the contributors to this exciting collection have a range of opinions about not only possible answers but also the validity of the questions themselves. The breadth and depth of scholarship that is employed in getting to grips with them is inspiring and exciting – a clear indication of the ways in which feminist scholarship has come of age in the last twenty years. And, indeed, the serious academic positions and honours of the scholars who have contributed to this collection are a further indication of feminist entrenchment in the academy to a degree that would have seemed almost unthinkable two decades ago. However, only Chandra Talpade Mohanty, among the contributors, directly raises the question of the implications of her own/other feminists' location in particular institutional structures before she turns to the political implications of the coincidence of interest among feminist and anti-racist/Third World postcolonial studies in questions of difference and political commonalities.

The editors each contributed a chapter – one at the beginning and one at the end. Anne Phillips, whose paper is the first substantive chapter, contributes a polished and now-familiar critique of the universal, masculinist assumptions embedded in conventional liberal political theory. Michele Barrett closes the book with a careful reflective piece on the cultural, 'deconstructive' turn in feminist theorizing. Barrett's final chapter is preceded by a paper by Gayatri Chakravorty Spivak in which she also addresses questions about language and meaning in an uncharacteristically accessible essay about the politics of location between cultures which is partly based on a conversation with Barrett. This chapter stimulated me to return to Spivak's earlier work which I find difficult to understand.

The other contributors range widely across contemporary debates, from key issues in social and political theory (the chapters by Walby and by Pringle and Watson), through theories of sexual identity and the body (Martin and Gatens), to questions about meaning and representation in painting (Pollock) as well as in text. Sadly the editors did not provide a concluding 'pulling together' final chapter so the reader is left to sort out for herself where the authors agree and disagree but it is an absorbing task. It should not surprise those familiar with Sylvia Walby's growing body of work on patriarchy that she is perhaps the most wedded to the continued relevance of pre-postmodern (or is post-postmodern as she hints in her title) theoretical structures, continuing an argument she has begun elsewhere about the transition between different forms of patriarchy. Her antagonism to discourse theory nicely sets the scene for other authors to disagree with her and this they do in a fascinating *mélange* of different styles and approaches. Coming immediately after Walby's measured academic style, the opening of the next chapter, in which Rosemary Pringle and Sophie Watson recount a dream one of them had, comes as quite a surprise. In an interesting paper, they go on to argue that postmodern or poststructuralist thought, more commonly discussed in the arena of cultural politics, may be relevant to the development of feminist approaches to the state.

But to single out particular chapters is invidious. All the contributions are interesting. Most of them are 'tasters' or summaries of more complex bodies of work published elsewhere in more detail. Gatens, for example, ranges widely in a few brief pages over theories of power, difference and the body, whereas Pollock manages both to distil and expand some of the arguments of her earlier collection, *Visions of Difference*, in a provocative essay that is nicely illustrated (thanks Polity for not bumping the price up by too much). The chapters hum with passion and excitement. Their authors display an enviable grasp of contemporary critical theory and yet, in the limited space allocated to them, they manage to deal with complex issues about discourse, language and representation in a clear, succinct and relatively accessible way. This collection should thus play an important part in introducing these debates to the uninitiated, the sceptical and those without much time! Hopefully, however, everybody who reads these short chapters will be persuaded to turn to other sources that explore similar issues in more detail.

If I had a quibble with the overall emphasis of the collection, however, it would be that the sheer intellectual thrills of the book tend to outweigh discussion of the political implications of contemporary theoretical destabilization. This is not to deny, of course, the political significance of the deconstruction and reconstruction of knowledge but rather to ask for clearer views about the ways in which we might build on our commonalities as well as try to understand our differences: ways in which we might move towards what Mohanty calls here 'engagement rather than discovery'. But perhaps this might be the subject of a second collection: hopefully as stimulating as this first one.

Linda McDowell

LETTER

Dear Feminist Review,

I am writing in response to 'Lesbian Romance Fiction' by Joke Hermes which appeared in *Feminist Review* 42 Autumn 1992. As a post-graduate student (Warwick University) looking at the lesbian pulps that were published throughout the 1950s/60s I was more than pleased to read something critical about the genre. It is an area of popular culture with a lot to offer in terms of lesbian culture/subject relations and one that has not received much critical attention. For what it's worth I would like to offer some thoughts around, what I, for one, would like to see as an ongoing debate in terms of how these texts can be assessed.

Hermes states that she wants lesbian romance without politics. She feels 'that fiction isn't the best means of political education'. Further she stresses that 'as a reader, I feel that political education spoils a good romance' (p. 51) But isn't all fiction political? The crop of feminist readings of heterosexual romance some ten years ago, if nothing else, demonstrated that a previously maligned site of women's reading pleasure contained a mass of politics – not only in terms of what had been classist dismissal but also in terms of sexual politics. Similarly, we might well consider the problems inherent in ever trying to view 'pleasure' as an a-political area – especially in the light of 1) debates between pro-pleasure and pro-censorship feminists and 2) the arguments that continue to rage inside and outside of feminist thought around Freudian proposals concerning pleasure and its ramifications.

Hermes takes exception to the narrative inclusion of the worst rapacious excesses of men as portrayed in *Stranger on Lesbos* and the more recent *Emergence of Green*. She does not feel 'that terrible childhoods (incestuous rape) or brutal husbands make a good case for lesbianism' (64). This raises several questions. First, does that mean that lesbians with such a history have arrived at their sexual preference by dint of that kind of past alone? Do we therefore place their lesbianism as less significant or as somehow less authentic for those women who choose lesbianism without such a past? What might lesbian readers with such a past obtain from these texts? Such questions are not raised because the concern of this critic is to give an individual reading. I also found the attempt at conflating the roles of critic and reader at once fascinating and problematic.

When does a reader become a critic – or, in this case, when does the critic Hermes become romance reader Hermes? Claiming pleasure as her mean appears to be Hermes the reader but when she argues a case against politics in the narrative is that a reader's preference or a critical stance? One thing is clear and that is positioning herself as 'reader' allows her to rail against 'outright social criticism' in lesbian romances because 'there is no way, whether in lesbian or in heterosexual romances that rape and moralizing will give me any amount of reading pleasure' (p. 65). Well, that is her choice and although she has every right to state her case to those who may be writing, or thinking about writing, such narratives, what do we do with those lesbian paperbacks – especially those from the 1950s/60s – that do have a discernible morality? And I don't just mean 'moral' in relation to sexual politics. Lesbian pulp paperbacks like *That Other Hunger* (1964) by Sloane Britain, for example, give an early popular fictional critique of the excessive use of hard drugs. *That Unfortunate Flesh* (1960) by Randy Salem has one protagonist portray the character deterioration that can accompany the expectation of inherited wealth. *Mavis* (1953) by Justin Kent plays itself out against a backdrop of small radio station versus takeover bid from a monopolist. In this way these 50s/60s paperbacks engage with sets of American morals and so provide socio-economic, ideological and historical comment and commentary that makes for a symbiotic link between fiction and culture. Hermes is welcome to ignore the social criticism in such texts and to seek out those texts that give her the kind of pleasure that she wants but. . .

With such little published on this form of writing I would not like the particular reading preference of Hermes to become a clarion call for a mass dismissal of – especially 1950/60s – lesbian paperbacks that use fiction to critique, amongst other issues, the very real excesses and abuses of some heterosexual practices and/or negative representations of lesbianism. Her emphasis on 'the political stance of the author' (p. 64) as a discernible reason to steer clear of certain texts conveniently forgets the interpretative power of reader response – other than her own. Which brings me to my own research in this area. . .

Only a favoured few of these pulps from the past have been reprinted and many of the thousands produced – 1950–1970 – have long since vanished. Part of my own research is attempting to look at the impact these paperbacks had on lesbian readers from the UK. Interviews already completed show signs of giving a complex picture. I have until the end of June 1993 to track down and interview respondents. If you read them at any time in the 1950s/60s or know anybody that did – and would be prepared to be interviewed – please contact me:

Carol Ann Uszkurat
PO Box 2013
London E17 9EW

AUDRE LORDE
1934–1992

As we were going to press with this issue we learned of the death of Audre Lorde. Knowledge of her fourteen-year fight against cancer could not lessen our distress and sadness. It is hard to be reconciled to the loss of her voice and to no longer having her generous and perceptive insights. We will publish an appreciation of her enormous contribution to feminism in a subsequent issue.

PHOTOGRAPH: INGRID POLLARD

NOTICEBOARD

New publications

Alternative Press Index
The Alternative Press Center, publisher of the quarterly, the *Alternative Press Index*, is pleased to announce the publication of its first annual cumulative index for Volume 23, 1991. Nearly 400 pages in length, it features over 36,000 citations covering 216 unique publications. This edition also features a list of periodicals indexed complete with subscription information.

The *Alternative Press Index* is the most complete index in the United States to the periodicals that offer a perspective not found in the mainstream press. This is a comprehensive guide to alternative, progressive and radical periodicals – in both popular and academic form. Some of the publications covered include *Race and Class, Labor Notes, Earth Island Journal, Gay Community News, Index on Censorship, New Left Review* and *Women's Studies Quarterly* – and many more.

Articles are indexed by subject heading in a format similar to the *Readers' Guide to Periodical Literature*. Subject headings, more than 5,000 in all, have been developed independently and reflect current terminology. A wide variety of subjects are covered including the environment, feminism, the gay and lesbian movement, political parties, multiculturalism, the media, international relations and social theory.

The cumulative index for Volume 23, 1991 is available from the Alternative Press Center, PO Box 33109, Baltimore, MD, 21218 (Tel: 410 243 2471). The price is $50 through December 1992, with a special discount for individual, non-profit and movement groups. Call or write for more information.

UCG Women's Studies Centre Review
UCG Women's Studies Centre Review, Byrne, A., J. Conroy and S. Ryder, editors, UCG WSC, Galway, 1992, viii–132 pp., 13 pl., 3 fig., pbk. £6 (lr.) ISBN 0 951 94660 9

The Women's Studies Centre in University College Galway organizes teaching and research, including seminars and conferences, in the many areas covered by gender studies.

The first volume of the *UCG Women's Studies Centre Review* was published in May 1992. It contains three sections: Women in Irish Society, Women's History, Women and the Arts. The topics range from 'Women in Ancient Europe' to 'Irish women scientists', from 'The Irish travelling woman' to 'Women in Latin American writing'. Its contents are of interest to a mixed public of general readers, students and specialists.

The *UCG Women's Studies Centre Review* is available from major Irish booksellers and most University bookshops, or from the Secretary, The Women's Studies Centre, c/o the Archway, University College, Galway, Ireland. Tel: 091 24411, ext. 3035/3009; Fax: 091 25700. Telex: 091 28823. Price £7 (including p&p) to Ireland and the UK, or $20 (including p&p) to Transatlantic and Continental addresses.

Future issues will appear annually. Each will be a separate and independent publication.

Fair Interviewing
Fair Interviewing is a handbook produced by Annie Hedge and Barbara Darling to help organizations ensure that they appoint the right applicants for the right posts. It details procedures to help you find out what applicants are capable of and to help you make the most appropriate selection.

Available from Trentham Books, Westview House, 734, London Road, Oakhill, Stoke-on-Trent, ST4 5NP, England. £8–95. ISBN 0 948 08080 9.

Women, Ink.
Women, Ink is a new project jointly established by the United Nations Development Fund for Women and the International Women's Tribune Centre to market and distribute women and development materials. It has just produced two new publications: *Freedom From Violence: Women's Strategies From Around the World* and *Legal Literacy: A Tool For Women's Empowerment.*

Available from Women, Ink. 777 United Nations Plaza, New York, NY 10017, USA.

Exhibition

Women and Design Between the Wars
A group of academic staff in the Faculty of Art, Design and Humanities

at the University of Brighton is involved in organizing an exhibition on 'Women and Design Between the Wars' for the University Gallery and other venues, to take place in March 1994. We have adopted an approach to the exhibition which will encompass a wide variety of design areas, aiming to give a view of women's achievements which challenges notions of what designers were actually involved in, and the ways in which they worked.

A feature of the exhibition is intended to be something in the nature of a 'roll of honour' to include the names of as many female designers as can be discovered. If any of your readers have names of designers they think should be included, we would be interested and grateful to hear from them. Any contributions to the exhibition will, of course, be fully acknowledged.

For those who might wish to share their knowledge of this subject in a more direct way, we are hoping to organize a conference/day school to coincide with the exhibition and would welcome proposals for papers.

Contact: Suzette Worden or Jill Seddon, School of Historical and Critical Studies, Faculty of Art, Design and Humanities, University of Brighton, Grand Parade, Brighton, BN2 2JY, England.

Helpline

Women's Nationwide Cancer Control Campaign has a Helpline from 9.30 am to 4.30 pm Monday to Friday to answer questions about breast checks, smear tests, colposcopy. Tel: 071 729 2229. 24-hour tapes are available on Breast Awareness 071 729 4915 and on Cervical Screening 071-729-5061.

You can also write to them: Helpline, WNCCC, Suna House, 128/130 Curtain Road, London EC2A 3AR.

Appeal for feminist books/journals

South Emsall is a declining mining area. The local pit, Frickley, was one of the thirty-one pits originally threatened for closure. For the first time ever in this area women are being offered the opportunity to study in the community for a degree. A group of sixteen women are working for the Certificate in Higher Education and most of them will go on to complete their degrees at Leeds Metropolitan University (formerly the poly). The course is a real morale booster in the area. The students are keen – some are single mothers, some are the wives of miners or ex-miners and many are hoping to improve their employment prospects for when the recession ends. They are, however, desperately short of books. They have been given a small sum from Wakefield Council to spend on new books and they have received a few donations of old sociology books. They would be overjoyed to receive feminist books and journals if you have any old or spare copies.

Send your donations to Wendy Formby, c/o Westfield Enterprise and Resource Centre, Westfield Lane, South Emsall, near Pontefract, West Yorkshire. For further information contact Wendy on 0977 674840.

Women's Studies Network (UK) Annual Conference 16–18 July 1993

Stirring It - Uniting Theory and Practice
Call for papers

Proposals are invited for papers for the Women's Studies Network (UK) Annual Conference, **Stirring It - Uniting Theory and Pactice**, to be held 16–18 July 1993 at Nene College, Northampton, for the following conference strands:

1) Violence
2) Lesbians in Theory
3) Women's Studies, Ethnic Studies, Black Studies
4) Women and Religions
5) Women and Cultural Production
6) Managing Women

The Women's Studies Network (UK) particularly welcomes papers by women from diverse ethnic backgrounds, disabled women, lesbians and students for all six strands.

Full wheelchair access.

For further information about the conference strands, write to:

Gabriele Griffin, Dept. of English, Nene College, Moulton Park, Northampton NN2 7AL.

Feminist Review

Since its founding in 1979 **Feminist Review** has been the major Women's Studies journal in Britain. **Feminist Review** is committed to presenting the best of contemporary feminist analysis, always informed by an awareness of changing political issues. The journal is edited by a collective of women based in London, with the help of women and groups from all over the United Kingdom.

● WHY NOT SUBSCRIBE? MAKE SURE OF YOUR COPY

All subscriptions run in calendar years. The issues for 1993 are Nos. 43, 44 and 45. You will save over £6 pa on the single copy price.

● SUBSCRIPTION RATES, 1993 (3 issues)

Individual Subscriptions

UK/EEC	£21
Overseas	£28
North America	$46

A number of reduced cost (£15.50 per year: UK only) subscriptions are available for readers experiencing financial hardship, e.g. unemployed, student, low-paid. If you'd like to be considered for a reduced subscription, please write to the Collective, c/o the Feminist Review office, 11 Carleton Gardens, Brecknock Road, London N19 5AQ.

Institutional Subscriptions		**Back Issues**	
UK	£56	UK	£8.99
Overseas	£62	North America	$16.50
North America	$100		

☐ Please send me one year's subscription to **Feminist Review**

☐ Please send me_____copies of back issue no._____

METHOD OF PAYMENT

☐ I enclose a cheque/international money order to the value of_____
 made payable to Routledge Journals

☐ Please charge my Access/Visa/American Express/Diners Club account

Account no. ☐☐☐☐☐☐☐☐☐☐☐☐☐☐☐☐☐☐

Expiry date_____ Signature_____

If the address below is different from the registered address of your credit card, please give your registered address separately.

PLEASE USE BLOCK CAPITALS

Name_____

Address_____

_____Postcode_____

☐ Please send me a Routledge Journals Catalogue

☐ Please send me a Routledge Gender and Women's Studies Catalogue

Please return this form with payment to:
Trevina White, Routledge Journals, Cheriton House, North Way, Andover, Hants SP10 5BE

BACK ISSUES

29 ABORTION: THE INTERNATIONAL AGENDA: Whatever Happened to 'A Woman's Right to Choose'?, **Berer**. More than 'A Woman's Right to Choose'?, **Himmelweit**. Abortion in the Republic of Ireland, **Barry**. Across the Water, **Irish Women's Abortion Support Group**. Spanish Women and the Alton Bill, **Spanish Women's Abortion Support Group**. The Politics of Abortion in Australia: Freedom, Church and State, **Coleman**. Abortion in Hungary, **Szalai**. Women and Population Control in China: Issues of Sexuality, Power and Control, **Hillier**. The Politics of Abortion in Nicaragua: Revolutionary Pragmatism – or Feminism in the Realm of Necessity?, **Molyneux**. Who Will Sing for Theresa?, **Bernstein**. She's Gotta Have It: The Representation of Black Female Sexuality on Film, **Simmonds**. Poems, **Gallagher**. Dyketactics for Difficult Times: A Review of the 'Homosexuality, Which Homosexuality?' Conference, **Franklin & Stacey**

30 Capital, Gender and Skill: Women Homeworkers in Rural Spain, **Lever**. Fact and Fiction: George Egerton and Nellie Shaw, **Butler**. Feminist Political Organization in Iceland: Some Reflections on the Experience of Kwenna Frambothid, **Dominelli & Jonsdottir**. Under Western Eyes: Feminist Scholarship and Colonial Discourses, **Talpade Mohanty**. Bedroom Horror: The Fatal Attraction of *Intercourse*, **Merck**. AIDS: Lessons from the Gay Community, **Patton**. Poems, **Agbabi**.

31 THE PAST BEFORE US: 20 YEARS OF FEMINISM: Slow Change or No Change?: Feminism, Socialism and the Problem of Men, **Segal**. There's No Place Like Home: On the Place of Identity in Feminist Politics, **Adams**. New Alliances: Socialist-Feminism in the Eighties, **Harriss**. Other Kinds of Dreams, **Parmar**. Complexity, Activism, Optimism: Interview with **Angela Y. Davis**. To Be or Not To Be: The Dilemmas of Mothering, **Rowbotham**. Seizing Time and Making New: Feminist Criticism, Politics and Contemporary Feminist Fiction, **Lauret**. Lessons from the Women's Movement in Europe, **Haug**. Women in Management, **Coyle**. Sex in the Summer of '88, **Ardill & O'Sullivan**. Younger Women and Feminism, **Hobsbawm & Macpherson**. Older Women and Feminism, **Stacey; Curtis; Summerskill**.

32 'Those Who Die for Life Cannot Be Called Dead': Women and Human Rights Protest in Latin America, **Schirmer**. Violence Against Black Women: Gender, Race and State Responses, **Mama**. Sex and Race in the Labour Market, **Breugel**. The 'Dark Continent': Africa as Female Body in Haggard's Adventure Fiction, **Stott**. Gender, Class and the Welfare State: The Case of Income Security in Australia, **Shaver**. Ethnic Feminism: Beyond the Pseudo-Pluralists, **Gorelick**.

33 Restructuring the Woman Question: *Perestroika* and Prostitution, **Waters**. Contemporary Indian Feminism, **Kumar**. 'A Bit On the Side'?: Gender Struggles in South Africa, **Beall, Hassim and Todes**. 'Young Bess': Historical Novels and Growing Up, **Light**. Madeline Pelletier (1874–1939): The Politics of Sexual Oppression, **Mitchell**.

34 PERVERSE POLITICS: LESBIAN ISSUES
Pat Parker: A tribute, **Brimstone**. International Lesbianism: Letter from São Paulo, **Rodrigues**; Israel, **Pittsburgh**, Italy, **Fiocchetto**. The De-eroticization of Women's Liberation: Social Purity Movements and the Revolutionary Feminism of Sheila Jeffreys, **Hunt**. Talking About It: Homophobia in the Black Community, **Gomez & Smith**. Lesbianism and the Labour Party, **Tobin**. Skirting the Issue: Lesbian Fashion for the 1990s, **Blackman & Perry**. Butch/Femme Obsessions, **Ardill & O'Sullivan**. Archives: The Will to Remember, **Nestle**; International Archives, **Read**. Audre Lorde: Vignettes and Mental Conversations, **Lewis**. Lesbian Tradition, **Field**. Mapping: Lesbians, AIDS and Sexuality An interview with Cindy Patton, **O'Sullivan**. Significant Others: Lesbians and Psychoanalytic Theory, **Hamer**. The Pleasure Threshold: Looking at Lesbian Pornography on Film, **Smyth**. Cartoon, **Charlesworth**. Voyages of the Valkyries: Recent Lesbian Pornographic Writing, **Dunn**.

35 Campaign Against Pornography, **Norden**. The Mothers' Manifesto and Disputes over 'Mütterlichkeit', **Chamberlayne**. Multiple Mediations: Feminist Scholarship in the Age of Multi-National Reception, **Mani**. Cagney and Lacey Revisited, **Alcock & Robson**. Cutting a Dash: The Dress of Radclyffe Hall and Una Troubridge, **Rolley**. Deviant Dress, **Wilson**. The House that Jill Built: Lesbian Feminist Organizing in Toronto, 1976–1980, **Ross**. Women in Professional Engineering: the Interaction of Gendered Structures and Values, **Carter & Kirkup**. Identity Politics and the Hierarchy of Oppression, **Briskin**. Poetry: **Bufkin, Zumwalt**.

36 'The Trouble Is It's Ahistorical': The Problem of the Unconscious in Modern Feminist Theory, **Minsky**. Feminism and Pornography, **Ellis, O'Dair, Tallmer**. Who Watches the Watchwomen? Feminists Against Censorship, **Rodgerson & Semple**. Pornography and Violence: What the 'Experts' Really Say, **Segal**. The Woman In My Life: Photography of Women, **Nava**. Splintered Sisterhood: Antiracism in a Young Women's Project, **Connolly**. Woman, Native, Other, **Parmar** interviews **Trinh T. Minh-ha**. Out But Not Down: Lesbians' Experience of Housing, **Edgerton**. Poems: **Evans Davies, Tóth, Weinbaum**. Oxford Twenty Years On: Where Are We Now?, **Gamman & O'Neill**. The Embodiment of Ugliness and the Logic of Love: The Danish Redstockings Movement, **Walter**.

37 THEME ISSUE: WOMEN, RELIGION AND DISSENT
Black Women, Sexism and Racism: Black or Antiracist Feminism?, **Tang Nain**. Nursing Histories: Reviving Life in Abandoned Selves, **McMahon**. The Quest for National Identity: Women, Islam and the State in Bangladesh, **Kabeer**. Born Again Moon: Fundamentalism in Christianity and the Feminist Spirituality Movement, **McCrickard**. Washing our Linen: One Year of Women Against Fundamentalism, **Connolly. Siddiqui** on *Letter to Christendom*, **Bard** on *Generations of Memories*, **Patel** on *Women Living Under Muslim Laws Dossiers 1–6*, Poem, **Kay**. More Cagney and Lacey, **Gamman**.

38 The Modernist Style of Susan Sontag, **McRobbie**. Tantalizing Glimpses of Stolen Glances: Lesbians Take Photographs, **Fraser and Boffin**. Reflections on the Women's Movement in Trinidad, **Mohammed**. Fashion, Representation and Femininity, **Evans & Thornton**. The European Women's Lobby, **Hoskyns**. **Hendessi** on *Law of Desire: Temporary Marriage in Iran*, **Kaveney** on *Mercy*.

39 SHIFTING TERRITORIES: FEMINISM & EUROPE
Between Hope and Helplessness: Women in the GDR, **Dölling**. Where Have All the
Women Gone? Women and the Women's Movement in East Central Europe,
Einhorn. The End of Socialism in Europe – A New Challenge For Socialist
Feminism? **Haug**. The Second 'No': Women in Hungary, **Kiss**. The Citizenship
Debate: Women, the State and Ethnic Processes, **Yuval-Davis**. Fortress Europe
and Migrant Women, **Morokvasíc**. Racial Equality and 1992, **Dummett**.
Questioning *Perestroika*: A Socialist Feminist Interrogation, **Pearson**.
Postmodernism and its Discontents, **Soper**. **Feminists and Socialism:** After the
Cold War, **Kaldor**. Socialism Out of the Common Pots, **Mitter**. 1989 and All That,
Campbell. In Listening Mode, **Cockburn**. **Women in Action: Country by
Country:** The Soviet Union; Yugoslavia; Czechoslovakia; Hungary; Poland.
Reports: International Gay and Lesbian Association: Black Women and Europe
1992.

40 Fleurs du Mal or Second-Hand Roses?: Nathalie Barney, Romaine Brooks, and the
'Originality of the Avant-Garde', **Elliott & Wallace**. Poem, **Tyler-Bennett**.
Feminism and Motherhood: An American Reading, **Snitow**. Qualitative Research,
Appropriation of the 'Other' and Empowerment, **Opie**. Disabled Women and the
Feminist Agenda, **Begum**. Postcard From the Edge: Thoughts on the 'Feminist
Theory: An International Debate' Conference at Glasgow University, July 1991,
Radstone. Review Essay, **Munt**.

41 Editorial. The Selling of HRT: Playing on the Fear Factor, **Worcester & Whatley**.
The Cancer Drawings of Catherine Arthur, **Sebastyen**. Ten Years of Women's
Health 1982–92, **James**. AIDS Activism: Women and AIDS Activism in Victoria,
Australia, **Mitchell**. A Woman's Subject, **Friedli**. HIV and the Invisibility of
Women: Is there a Need to Redefine AIDS?, **Scharf & Toole**. Lesbians Evolving
Health Care: Cancer and AIDS, **Winnow**. Now is the Time for Feminist Criticism:
A Review of *Asinimali!*. **Steinberg** Ibu or the Beast: Gender Interests in Two
Indonesian Women's Organizations, **Wieringa**. Reports on Motherlands:
Symposium on African, Carribean and Asian Women's Writing, **Smart**. The
European Forum of Socialist Feminists, **Bruegel**. Review Essay, **Gamman**.

42 FEMINIST FICTIONS: Editorial. Angela Carter's *The Bloody Chamber* and the
Decolonization of Feminine Sexuality, **Makinen**. Feminist Writing: Working with
Women's Experience, **Haug**. Three Aspects of Sex in Marge Piercy's *Fly Away
Home*, **Hauser**. Are They Reading Us? Feminist Teenage Fiction, **Bard**. Sexuality
in Lesbian Romance Fiction, **Hermes**. A Psychoanalytic Account for Lesbianism,
Castendyk. Mary Wollstonecraft and the Problematic of Slavery, **Ferguson**.
Reviews.

43 ISSUES FOR FEMINISM: Family, Motherhood and Zulu Nationalism: The
Politics of the Inkatha Women's Brigade, **Hassim**. Postcolonialism, Feminism and
the Veil: Thinking the Difference, **Abu Odeh**. Feminism, the Menopause and
Hormone Replacement Therapy, **Lewis**. Feminism and Disability, **Morris**. 'What
is Pornography?': An Analysis of the Policy Statement of the Campaign Against
Pornography and Censorship, **Smith**. Reviews.

Women, Theory, Fiction

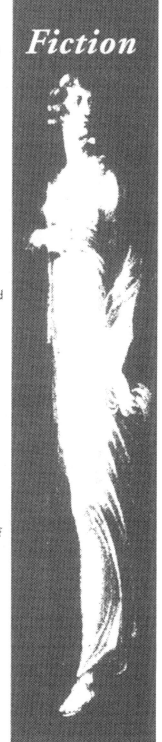

Je, Tu, Nous

Towards a Culture of Difference

Luce Irigaray

Translated by **Alison Martin**

In a series of brief and direct essays on the position of women in the modern world, Luce Irigaray offers the clearest exposition available of her own radical philosophy.

' A powerful contribution to feminist scholarship' – *Judith Butler*

March 1993 122pp Hb £30 Pb £7.99

(Un)like Subjects

Women, Theory, Fiction

Gerardine Meaney

Gerardine Meaney traces the connections between Cixous, Irigaray and Kristeva, and Lessing, Spark and Carter, in a stunning work on the relationships within and between women's writing.

June 1993 288pp Hb £35.00 Pb £10.99

Contemporary Feminist Theatres

To Each Her Own

Lizbeth Goodman

A sophisticated and innovative evaluation of the forms feminism has taken in the theatre since 1968. A landmark study of political theatre and practical feminism.

March 1993 328pp Hb £35.00 Pb £11.99

Decolonizing Feminisms

Race, Gender and Empire Building

Laura E. Donaldson

Combining readings of literature, films and critical theory, Laura Donaldson situates contemporary theoretical debates about reading, writing and the politics of identity within the context of historical colonialism.

March 1993 184pp Hb £35.00 Pb £9.99

Marguerite Duras

Apocalyptic Desires

Leslie Hill

'Hill takes us into the heartlands of Duras' self-promotional mythology and analyses her work in a variety of media with astonishing dexterity and confidence.' – *Malcolm Bowie*

July 1993 288pp Hb £35.00 Pb £11.99

Routledge, 11 New Fetter Lane, London EC4P 4EE
and 29 West 35th Street,
New York, NY 10001

GENDER
on anthropology

Gendered Anthropology

Edited by **Teresa del Valle**

A thought-provoking and lively examination of current debates focusing on sex, gender, race, ethnicity, politics and economics providing insights which are still often lacking in mainstream anthropology.

Contributors include
Henrietta Moore, Marianne Gullestad, Marit Melhuus and Signe Howell, Serge Tcherkezoff, Verena Stolcke, Sabine Strasser and Hildergard Diemberger.

The European Association of Social Anthropologists Series

June 1993: 216x138: 224pp: illus. 6 b+w photographs
Hb: 0-415-06126-1: £35.00   Pb: 0-415-06127-X: £11.99

Gendered Fields

Women, Men and Ethnography

Edited by **Diane Bell**, **Pat Caplan**
and **Wazir Jahan Karim**

Highlights the effects of the gender of the anthropologist on the process of fieldwork. Contributors offer an international perspective on gender, knowledge and power with a view to achieving greater sensitivity and a major rethinking of future fieldwork approaches.

March 1993: 234x156: 272pp: illus. 12 b+w photographs and 2 maps
Hb: 0-415-06251-9: £40.00   Pb: 0-415-06252-7: £14.99

DIVINE
DECADENCE

°Fascism, Female Spectacle, and
the Makings of Sally Bowles

LINDA MIZEJEWSKI

As femme fatale, cabaret siren, and icon of Camp, Sally Bowles has become this century's darling of "divine decadence." Originally a character in a short story by Christopher Isherwood, published in 1939, "Sally" has appeared over the years in the stage play *I Am a Camera*, the film of the same name, and a stage musical and Academy Award-winning musical film, both entitled *Cabaret*.

Linda Mizejewski shows how each successive repetition of the tale of the showgirl and the male writer has linked the young man's fascination with Sally more closely to the fascination of fascism. To Mizejewski, the adaptations end up duplicating the fascist politics they strain to condemn, reproducing the homophobia, misogyny, fascination for spectacle, and emphasis of sexual difference that characterized German fascism. This interdisciplinary work breaks new ground in gender studies.

Paper: £10.95 ISBN 0-691-02346-8   Cloth: £25.00 ISBN 0-691-07896-3
Due Spring 1993

ORDER FROM YOUR BOOKSELLER OR FROM

Princeton University Press

C/O JOHN WILEY & SONS, 1 OLDLANDS WAY, BOGNOR REGIS, WEST SUSSEX, PO22 9SA